Chimney Swifts

Number Thirty-seven:

Louise Lindsey Merrick Natural Environment Series

Chimney Swifts

America's Mysteriou

Birds above the Fireplace

by PAUL D. KYLE and GEORGEAN Z. KYLE

Illustrated by Georgean Z. Kyle
Photography by Paul D. Kyle

TEXAS A&M UNIVERSITY PRESS
College Station

The paper used in this book
meets the minimum requirements
of the American National Standard for Permanence
of Paper for Printed Library Materials, Z39.48-1984.
Binding materials have been chosen for durability.
∞

Library of Congress Cataloging-in-Publication Data

Kyle, Paul D., 1950–
    Chimney swifts / America's mysterious birds above the
fireplace / by Paul D. Kyle and Georgean Z. Kyle ; photography by Paul D. Kyle.—1st ed.
        p. cm.—(Louise Lindsey Merrick natural environment
series ; no. 37)
    Includes bibliographical references (p.) and index.
    ISBN 1-58544-370-0 (cloth : alk. paper)—
    ISBN 1-58544-371-9 (pbk. : alk. paper)
    1. Chimney swift. I. Kyle, Georgean Z., 1950–
II. Title. III. Series.
QL696.A552K952   2005
598.7'62—dc22   2004011777

Contents

Preface

WE MOVED TO AUSTIN, TEXAS, in 1973, purchased property in northwest Travis County, and began construction of our personally hand-built home. In 1974, we moved into the house while it was still under construction.

We immediately fell in love with the topography of the Texas Hill Country. Although our academic knowledge of the native flora and fauna was limited, we had an appreciation for the plethora of life that surrounded us both inside and outside our home. Canyon Wrens squeezed under the un-weather-stripped doors, the occasional Red-bellied Woodpecker hammered its way through the unfinished eaves, and White-tailed Deer, Eastern Cottontails, and Nine-banded Armadillos ravaged our attempts at gardening—but we delighted in the abundance of life around us.

Now and again we came across a fallen nestling or injured animal. So, when the Austin Nature Center offered a wildlife-rehabilitation class, we promptly enrolled. In 1982, we applied for and received our state and federal permits to rehabilitate protected native wildlife. One thing led to another, and in short order we found our small home filled with incubators and cages containing many species of injured, orphaned, and displaced wildlife. Porches were converted into bird flights, a room was remodeled to accommodate housing for nestlings, and the fenced garden became a pen for White-tailed Deer fawns.

We were introduced to our first Chimney Swift in early spring 1983 at the Travis County Humane

Society in Austin, Texas. Someone had found a small, sleek, black bird on the ground. It had apparently collided with a window and was unable to fly. The volunteer handed us a shoe box, and we carefully slid the top partially to the side. Instead of seeing the flurry of feathers, feet, and bill that we had come to expect from wild birds, we were confronted with the most remarkable eyes we had ever seen. When we carefully reached inside the box, the bird did not struggle. Instead, it willingly climbed on, clung tightly, gazed directly into our eyes for a few moments, then wearily closed its lids, and resigned itself to whatever fate was to come.

We were unsure of the species, but the bird was certainly unlike any other we had cared for previously. When we arrived home, we went straight to Peterson's field guide and confirmed that the bird was an adult Chimney Swift. Our rehabilitation reference materials indicated that this bird would require hand-feeding because the species has a unique physiology and because Chimney Swifts eat small flying insects caught in flight. After seventeen days of being force-fed a mealworm-based diet, the bird regained its health and was released. Since then, we have not been able to walk outside without looking up at the sky.

If the adult Chimney Swift was unusual, we thought the first brood of babies was absolutely bizarre. We were handed a small box that sounded as if it had been stuffed with mechanical windup toys. When it was opened, four reptilian-looking creatures exploded into a piercing "yipping" while bobbing and swaying their long necks. We were in love.

Our first attempts to hand-rear baby swifts had mixed results. Older, feathered birds survived but showed numerous developmental problems.

Adult Chimney Swift. It is not unusual for a hand-held Chimney Swift to linger briefly before flying to freedom.

Nestling Chimney Swift. The unusual appearance of young Chimney Swifts alone can be an incentive for their conservation.

"The line up." At feeding time, the fledgling swifts would line up along the top of their chimney. Here they were hand-fed mealworms every hour, twelve hours each day, until they were ready for release at five weeks of age.

Younger birds simply weakened and died after a few days. We began research to develop a Chimney Swift–specific diet. With the advice and suggestions of veterinary and nutritional professionals and the Texas A&M University Avian Diagnostic Laboratory, we were successful.

In 1984, our success in hand-rearing healthy Chimney Swifts was so much improved that we submitted our findings to the National Wildlife Rehabilitators Association (NWRA) for consideration. A subsequent invitation provided us an opportunity to present a paper at the 1985 NWRA symposium in Boston. At that national symposium, we accepted a grant to research our discovery of the apparent role of the saliva of adult Chimney Swifts in the proper development of their young.

Shortly after receiving our wildlife rehabilitation permits, we were issued U.S. Fish and Wildlife Service bird-banding permits. The permits enabled us to band all of our hand-reared birds for the purpose of evaluating our rehabilitation techniques. In 1989, we constructed our first two Chimney Swift towers. These structures made it possible to witness and record previously undocumented nesting and roosting behavior and to accumulate postrelease data. This documentation confirmed that we consistently raised healthy Chimney Swifts that were able to survive, migrate, and successfully breed in the wild. During our years as active wildlife rehabilitators, between 1982 and 1999, we provided care for fifteen hundred displaced and injured young and adult Chimney Swifts and wrote a detailed care guide enabling other avian rehabilitators nationwide to duplicate our rehabilitation success with Chimney Swifts.

From our first year of working with wildlife, we realized that public ignorance about and intolerance of wildlife was a major problem—especially regarding Chimney Swifts. Misinformed homeowners were reacting to raucous noises emanating from their fireplaces by lighting fires in an attempt to chase the unknown entities from their chimneys. The homeowners were horrified when they learned that they had set fire to hungry baby Chimney Swifts and their parents. In addition, the illegal activities of some professional chimney-

Hand-reared Chimney Swifts roosting. When the baby swifts were old enough to begin to fly, they were placed in an artificial chimney inside a large screened aviary. Here they would huddle closely just as swifts do in the wild.

cleaning companies were having a negative effect on the Chimney Swift population. Unfortunately, these activities continue even today, and Chimney Swifts are still declining in numbers.

We did our best to enlighten the public about Chimney Swifts. At first, we made just modest efforts to engage one person at a time. Later, with assistance from the Driftwood Wildlife Association, the Texas Partners in Flight program, and the Texas Parks and Wildlife Department, we produced two informational brochures: one for homeowners and one for professional chimney-cleaning companies. These were distributed nationally, and the concept of active Chimney Swift conservation began to spread.

In 1995, we received a private grant to establish the North American Chimney Swift Nest Site

Hand-reared Chimney Swifts flying. As they continued to develop their strength and confidence, the youngsters learned to fly in and out of their "chimney."

Research Project. This project has greatly expanded public awareness of the beneficial nature
as well as the plight of Chimney Swifts. The project
has attracted and inspired hundreds of research
associates all across North America who are, in
turn, constructing nesting towers and conducting
Chimney Swift conservation projects in their own
communities. In 1999, we proudly accepted a
National Partners in Flight award in Chicago for
our conservation and education efforts.

As others before us have done, we have observed, researched, hand-reared, and rehabilitated
Chimney Swifts. We have photographed, captured,
weighed, measured, and banded Chimney Swifts.
But because of the current state of our environment, we have had to do something with Chimney Swifts that few of our predecessors could have
possibly foreseen: we have had to become concerned about the fate of these small, unique birds.

During the twentieth century, much was discovered about the Chimney Swift. There were scien-
tific papers written and even a few books published
about this species' life and behavior. Chimney
Swifts had become so common and abundant that
fall roosts resembled smoke going back into chimneys. But by the late 1980s, when we became interested, Chimney Swifts—and many other
neotropical migrants—were in decline. From 1966
through 1991, the Chimney Swift population had
declined by 55.6 percent for the North American
continent as a whole.

According to the National Biological Service's
Breeding Bird Survey, Chimney Swift populations
were still declining in 1998. If the future of this
fascinating and beneficial species is to be a bright
one, more steps must be taken now. Their existing nesting and roosting habitat must be preserved
and not diminished. New habitat must be created

to replace habitat that has been lost. And most important, all of us in North America must come to know and understand these unique birds that raise their feathered families just above our fireplaces. For anyone who knows Chimney Swifts, the summer skies would seem desolate without the aerial antics and cheerful "chippering" sounds of these remarkable birds.

Paul and Georgean Kyle. The authors in front of the Pool Towers.
Courtesy Nancy Whitworth

Natural History and Biology

Chimney Swifts:

FAMILY: Apodidae

GENUS AND SPECIES: *Chaetura pelagica*

LENGTH: 5 inches (12.7 centimeters)

WINGSPAN: 12–12½ inches (31.75 centimeters)

WEIGHT: 0.8 ounce (22.8 grams)

COLOR: Sooty gray to bluish black with lighter gray throat; male and female identical in appearance

DESCRIPTION OF FLIGHT: Soar on long, scythe-shaped wings, stubby tail that spreads when turning sharply while feeding; abrupt, jerky, batlike flight that presents the illusion of wings flapping alternately (disproved)

VOICE: Adults: a sharp, rapid "tick-tick-tick" or bright "chippering" sound

Young feeding call: a raucous "gim-me, gim-me, gim-me"

Young alarm call: winding or whirring "raah, raah, raah"

DESCRIPTION AT REST: Unable to perch or stand; cling, facing upward, to vertical surfaces; center spines on tips of tail exposed like needles and prop against the vertical surface; long wings cross over the rump

TEMPORAL PRESENCE: Arrive in southern United States in mid-March; arrive in Canada by May; depart northernmost range by September and southernmost range by mid- to late October

RANGE: Winter: the upper Amazon basin of eastern Peru, northern Chile, and northwestern Brazil; full range unknown

Summer/breeding season: along the east coast of North America from southern Florida northward to Nova Scotia; westward from south Texas northward to southeastern Saskatchewan

NESTING PERIOD: May through August

NUMBER OF BROODS: Usually one and sometimes two in southern areas of breeding range

Vital Statistics

NEST: Twigs glued to the inside of a vertical shaft with saliva; built from locally available materials, such as small dead twigs or pine needles (an average nest contains about 265 individual pieces); built by both parents

WIDTH OF NEST: 3½–4¼ inches (8.9–10.8 centimeters)

HEIGHT OF NEST: 1–1¼ inches (2.5–3.1 centimeters)

Distance from the wall: 1⅞–3 inches (4.8–7.5 centimeters)

EGGS: 2–7; white (3–5 most common); ¾ x ½ inch (20.1 x 13.2 millimeters); 1.85 grams

INCUBATION: 18–21 days by both parents, alternating

BROODING OF YOUNG: By both parents, alternating

FEEDING OF YOUNG: By both parents on average every 30 minutes until the young are 7 days old; averaging hourly thereafter

NESTLINGS: Altricial (blind, naked, helpless) with proportionally large feet with sharp claws

  3 days: feather tracts visible

  10 days: wing feathers begin to unfurl

  14 days: eyes begin to open; milky blue in color; lids wrinkled

FLEDGLINGS: 20 days: eyes have turned brown; fully feathered; practice flapping

  21–26 days: flying up and down inside chimney or tower

  28–30 days: first flight outside chimney or tower

DIET: Primarily small flying insects less than 0.2 inch (5 millimeters) in length; insects taken include mosquitoes, midges, flies, spittlebugs, aphids, winged ants, tiny bees and wasps, mayflies, stoneflies, and termites; opportunistic feeders

LONGEVITY: Oldest known individual more than 14 years old

ECOLOGICAL STATUS: Numbers declining since mid-1980s

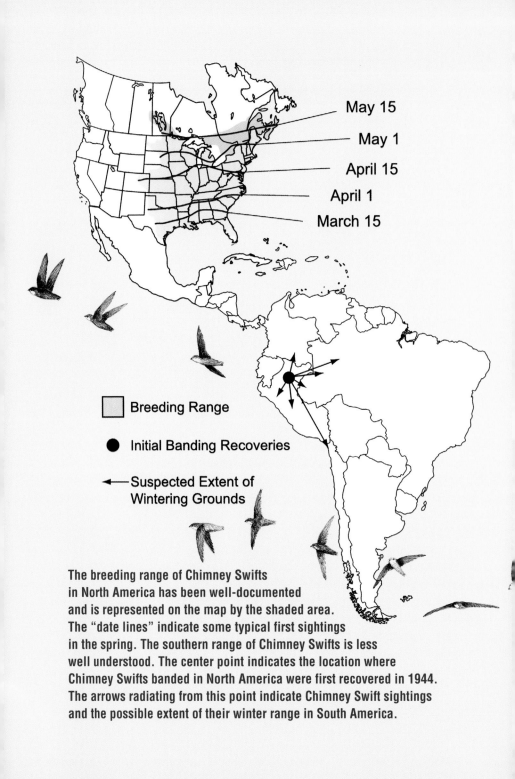

May 15
May 1
April 15
April 1
March 15

Breeding Range

Initial Banding Recoveries

Suspected Extent of
Wintering Grounds

The breeding range of Chimney Swifts
in North America has been well-documented
and is represented on the map by the shaded area.
The "date lines" indicate some typical first sightings
in the spring. The southern range of Chimney Swifts is less
well understood. The center point indicates the location where
Chimney Swifts banded in North America were first recovered in 1944.
The arrows radiating from this point indicate Chimney Swift sightings
and the possible extent of their winter range in South America.

An Introduction to Chimney Swifts

THERE ARE MORE THAN EIGHTY KNOWN species of swifts in the world. Of these, four species are commonly found in North America. The White-throated Swift (*Aeronautes saxatalis*) and Black Swifts (*Cypseloides niger*) inhabit the western part of the continent in mountainous and otherwise rugged areas. The Vaux's Swift (*Chaetura vauxi*) is most commonly found in the Pacific Northwest. The Chimney Swift (*Chaetura pelagica*: pronounced "kee-TOO-rah peh-LADGE-ih-kah") is the most common species of swift found east of the Rocky Mountains.

The summer skies are filled with many species of birds. However, none seem to be as much at home on the wing as Chimney Swifts. Even the graceful swallows must perch to preen and socialize, but Chimney Swifts flicker on, "chippering" and careening endlessly throughout the day.

The vocalizations of Chimney Swifts are as unique as they are difficult to accurately describe. Seldom are they referred to as melodic. They produce a sharp "ticking" call that is reminiscent of the sound of two stones being struck together rapidly and a "chippering" or "chattering" that is indescribable. Although to the human ear, the repertoire of notes may seem limited, variations in volume, frequency, and cadence give Chimney Swifts an impressive range of potential vocal expression.

Small, sleek, bluish black with silver gray throats, Chimney Swifts have been descriptively called "flying cigars" and "bows and arrows."

Other common names are chimney sweeps and chimney swallows.

Adult Chimney Swifts are most commonly seen in flight—usually in groups. Chimney Swifts may seem awkward or inept when attempting to leave the ground, but they are rarely in that situation. Their sleek design is a clear indication of how they perform when they are in their element of open sky. Their long, scythe-shaped wings span about 12.5 inches when soaring, supporting a proportionally short body with a squared-off tail that appears slightly rounded when spread. Their stiff, flickering movements alternate with long, graceful sweeps of flight as they scour the skies for flying

The tail and wings of a Chimney Swift.

insects to eat. The staccato, batlike flight when flapping their wings is due to short, relatively massive upper wing bones. An optical illusion created by the extremely rapid wing beats makes the wings appear to flap alternately—an aerodynamic impossibility. Even though stroboscopic photography disproved this illusion in 1950, every modern-day bird-watcher is impressed by it.

An average adult measures 5 inches in length and weighs 22.8 grams. Both sexes are identical in appearance. Each long, elegant wing contains ten primary or flight feathers. When Chimney Swifts are at rest, the wings cross by an inch or more over the tail feathers.

Perhaps the most distinctive physical feature of the Chimney Swift is its tail. The central shaft of each of the ten tail feathers ends in a sharp, exposed point. The genus name *Chaetura* has its derivation from the Greek *chaite,* meaning "stiff hair, bristle, or spine," and *oura,* meaning "tail": therefore, "spine-tailed." The only other species of bird in North America to have such a tail is the smaller Vaux's Swift, also in the genus *Chaetura.*

The feet and legs of the Chimney Swift are also unusual in that they are covered with delicate, smooth skin rather than scales. Chimney Swifts' feet are anisodactyl (three toes forward and one toe back), as are the feet of songbirds, but these swifts are able to shift the hallux (back toe, or claw) forward for a better grip. Their feet, legs, and tail have evolved to allow them to cling effortlessly to textured vertical surfaces when not in flight. This adaptation makes them unable to perch in the familiar songbird fashion and may give the mistaken impression that Chimney Swifts have "small, weak feet." They are members of the family Apodidae, which literally means "without feet." When forced to rest unnaturally on horizontal surfaces, Chimney

Swifts do assume a more or less prone position and seem rather helpless because they are unable to jump or "stand." In reality, their feet and legs are very strong. When roosting, they are able to support their entire body weight throughout the night with their grappling hook–like feet.

Speed, agility, and superior eyesight of the Chimney Swift are well complemented by its specialized mouth. The tiny bill belies an impressive gape that enables it to scoop flying insect prey from the air with ease. In upstate New York, Richard Fischer (1958) examined more than one thousand insects that he collected from the mouths of young swifts right after they had been fed by the parents. He found that insects taken by Chimney Swifts were seldom more than 0.2 in. long and that "at each visit a parent gave one nestling a pellet of food that, at times, contained more than 200 insects. . . . The chief food items in frequency of occurrence were Diptera [mosquitoes, midges, and flies], Homoptera [hoppers, spittle bugs, and aphids], Hymenoptera [ants, wasps, and bees], Ephemerida [mayflies] and Plecoptera [stoneflies]. These five orders accounted for approximately 95 percent of their [Chimney Swifts'] food. Other orders recorded were Coleoptera [beetles], Hemiptrera [bugs], Trichoptera [caddisflies] and Siphonaptera [fleas]. Spiders (Arachnida) were found on occasion" (p. 101).*

Page numbers in parentheses refer to the location of the quote in the reference cited. Reference section begins on page 137.

From samples that we have collected in Texas, we can corroborate Richard Fischer's findings and add Isoptera (termites) to the known diet of Chimney Swifts.

The aerial prowess of Chimney Swifts keeps them safe from most predators. Some swifts undoubtedly fall prey to falcons and other raptors, but they are truly vulnerable only when nesting and roosting. We have recorded predation of adults by raccoons, and eggs, young, and adults by rat snakes. Ants can also disrupt roosts and overrun nests. House cats have been observed lurking on or near chimneys where they catch swifts as the birds come and go from the site. Some species of owls will actually enter roosts after dark and pluck swifts from the walls. The only instances where we have ever observed Chimney Swifts flying at night have been the result of predators flushing birds from their roosts. Even small birds can present problems for nesting Chimney Swifts. We have witnessed "egg piercing" of unguarded eggs by clandestine Canyon Wrens.

The combined impact of all forms of natural predation probably pales when compared to the depredation that has been visited on Chimney Swifts by *Homo sapiens* since the swifts began to move from the forests to our chimneys.

A Chimney Swift's foot.

When *Chaetura pelagica* was first cataloged by early naturalists, it was given the common name American Swift. It was originally a resident of the woodlands of North America, mainly east of the Mississippi and the Missouri rivers, where it nested and roosted in large hollow trees. As European settlers began their movement across the continent, old-growth forests were cleared for agriculture, and much of the traditional swift habitat was destroyed.

Farms and towns quickly replaced the forests, and Chimney Swifts readily adapted to the countless brick and stone chimneys that were an integral part of the new construction boom. Swifts nested in the summer when fireplaces were not in use, so conflicts between the activities of birds and humans were rare. The new human-made habitat may have had advantages over hollow trees. Chimneys were more permanent and probably less susceptible to predation from other wildlife because of the proximity to humans.

The American Swift's rapid adaptation to chimneys (as well as to many other new structures, such as air shafts, wells, and outbuildings) was so successful that swifts dramatically expanded their range and numbers by following the human migration westward. Only the Rocky Mountains and the arid deserts of the American Southwest halted their expansion. By the end of the nineteenth century, swifts had become familiar summer residents in many midwestern urban areas, and the name was changed to suit the swifts' new lifestyle.

Even after the principles of bird migration were understood in many other species, the winter home of the Chimney Swift remained a mystery. In 1934 began what author Margaret Whittemore described as "the largest cooperative research project ever undertaken to trace the migratory path

A contemporary Chimney Swift nest site. Chimney Swifts now nest almost exclusively in human-made structures, such as masonry chimneys and industrial air shafts.
Photo by Leroy Williamson, courtesy Texas Parks and Wildlife © 2002

of a single species" (p. 57). Huge flocks of roosting Chimney Swifts were captured and banded in the spring and fall. Through the efforts of many individuals, hundreds of thousands of swifts were banded. Although dedicated researchers often handled several thousand swifts per day, Gordon L. Hight, Jr., of Rome, Georgia, holds the record with 7,377 swifts from a large commercial chimney in a single day.

The mystery was finally solved in 1943 when thirteen banded Chimney Swifts were "recovered" by indigenous residents of an unexplored tributary of the Amazon River in Peru. Albert F. Ganier detailed the event in the article "More about the Chimney Swifts Found in Peru" in the September 1944 edition of *The Migrant:* "The birds are reported to have been killed by Indians on the River Yanayaco, which is located in the region between the Putomayo and Napo Rivers. The bands were transmitted to the American Embassy at Lima by a student in the Library School of the National Library, who was given them by a friend, who in turn was presented them by the Indians" (p. 39).

When the bands were forwarded to the bird-banding laboratory in Laurel, Maryland, the winter home of the American Chimney Swifts was confirmed. All of the birds had been banded in the continental United States. Ben Coffey of Nashville, Tennessee, had banded five of the thirteen history-making birds. He ultimately banded more than 144,000 Chimney Swifts in his pursuit of knowledge about their migratory habits.

Chimney Swifts are now known to winter in the upper Amazon basin of eastern Peru, northern Chile, and northwestern Brazil. However, the full extent of their southern range is still unknown. Likewise, little is known about their behavior while they are on their wintering grounds.

Bird banding also helped ornithologists establish the known life span for Chimney Swifts. Richard Fischer analyzed extensive data from five different bird banders. He found that "few [Chimney] swifts live more than four years" (p. 44). The data also suggested an annual mortality rate of approximately 50 percent. And it is no wonder, considering the arduous migration of these little birds. A Chimney Swift that lives only one full year will fly as many as 10,000 miles solely in migration. However, some Chimney Swifts can and do live considerably longer than four years. Our own banding efforts have identified several individuals that lived longer, including one nine-year-old male that was tending a brood of six eggs with his mate.

R. W. Smith banded one of the oldest known Chimney Swifts at Kingston, Ontario, on May 18, 1940, when it was already more than one year old. Gordon Hight recaptured the same bird in Rome, Georgia, on September 25, 1952—confirming that the swift was more than thirteen years old. Ralph W. Dexter recovered an even older swift in 1969 that he had first banded fourteen years earlier in one of the air shafts at Kent State University in Kent, Ohio. By conservative calculations, that remarkable Chimney Swift had flown a minimum of 140,000 migration miles when it was released for the final time: the equivalent of more than five times around the equator.

Chimney Swifts begin their long journey north just as winter in the southern United States is giving way to the first rumors of spring. In mid- to late March, high overhead, they herald their arrival with distant, yet unmistakable, chippering. The birds are sighted almost simultaneously along the Gulf Coast of Texas, on the southern Atlantic coastline, and in Louisiana. This suggests that individuals choose between migration routes along the eastern Mexico coastline, island hopping across the Caribbean to Florida or flying directly across the Gulf of Mexico from their winter refuge in northwestern South America. Not all swifts migrate at the same time. Instead, they arrive as individuals or small groups, spanning a three-month period. In May 2000, Chimney Swifts were sighted simultaneously arriving in Nova Scotia and flying northward over an offshore drilling platform south of High Island, Texas.

Chimney Swifts rarely fly in a straight line for any length of time. Their preferred flight pattern consists of loops, swirls, and sweeping curves. Consequently, their annual one-way journey of greater than five thousand miles may easily be multiples of that distance. Because swifts regularly spend their entire day in the air, the journey may not be as diffIcult for them as it is for passerines (warblers, flycatchers, thrushes, etc.). They are, however, just as vulnerable to inclement weather as are all other migrants. Prevailing winds in spring generally blow southeasterly from the tropics, providing a tailwind advantage for the returning birds. Unfortunately, late-season cold fronts may arrive from the northwest, pushing well into the Gulf of Mexico and intercepting birds en route. The resulting flight conditions may include strong, gusty north winds, rain, and occasionally, hail. In addition to encountering tropical storms and hurricanes, migrants are subjected to starvation, exhaustion, and loss of familiar habitat for foraging and shelter. Other obstacles can include natural predators, hunters, and communication towers. To humans, it seems amazing that most individuals survive the gauntlet of migration.

By the first of May, Chimney Swifts grace the skies from the southernmost tip of both Texas and Florida north to Nova Scotia and from the east coast west to the Rocky Mountains. Over the summer months, they build their nests, raise their young, and delight the enlightened observer with their aerial acrobatics.

Chimney Swifts were originally residents of the eastern woodlands of North America, where they nested and roosted in large hollow trees.

Documenting the "Home Life" of Chimney Swifts

U NLIKE MANY AVIAN SPECIES that have been studied to the nth degree by multitudes of researchers, Chimney Swifts have drawn the attention of but a handful of dedicated investigators. The nesting and roosting activities typically take place in locations that are difficult to observe. Consequently, their terrestrial behavior has been accurately documented by only a few individuals. Not until 1915 was a means of closely studying these elusive birds developed.

Althea R. Sherman was one of the most diligent and persistent students of Chimney Swift nesting behavior in the twentieth century. Her extremely meticulous observations began when she was sixty-five years old. Her watchfulness spanned sixteen years (1918–34) and concluded only when her age and health prevented her from continuing. Fred J. Pierce reported: "Her day-to-day observations of Chimney Swifts filled two notebooks—a total of 400 pages and approximately 91,000 words written in longhand" (p. 61). Her book *Birds of an Iowa Dooryard* was edited by Fred Pierce and published posthumously in 1952. The third chapter, "The Home Life of the Chimney Swift," begins by explaining that she was fascinated and impressed by a paper written by Mary F. Day of New Jersey and published in 1899 in *Bird Lore*. Mary Day had apparently used a hand-held mirror inserted into a stovepipe hole of a chimney to observe and record the nest-building activities of a pair of Chimney Swifts. However, Althea Sherman notes that "many things were left unseen by her which better facilities for viewing might have revealed. Some of these things I am now able to describe" (p. 40).

In Althea Sherman's next paragraph, it becomes immediately apparent why she was able to make such detailed and accurate observations that few have surpassed to this day:

> Many years ago I planned a building which was not built until 1915. For lack of a better name, it is called the Chimney Swifts' tower. Its dimensions are 9 feet square and 28 feet to the top of the chimney. The artificial chimney is 2 feet square, and runs down the center of the tower to a depth of 14 feet; the chimney was built of pine flooring with the rough sides of the boards turned within. A door opens into the chimney and a stationary ladder may be climbed for closing and opening the top of the chimney in fall and spring, respectively. Auger-holes serve as peepholes on two sides, while on the other two sides are windows. The frames of these windows are not vertical but are in two planes which meet at an obtuse angle. Into this space which juts into the chimney one's head can be introduced, and through the glass a view to the bottom or to the top of the chimney may be obtained without unduly frightening the birds (p.40).

Ralph W. Dexter made a lifelong career of studying the swifts that nested and roosted in the air shafts of the buildings on the campus of Kent State University in Ohio where he was a member of the

This unique tower was the inspiration for modern-day conservation efforts on behalf of Chimney Swifts. The observations that Sherman made in the tower and detailed in her handwritten notes filled four hundred pages and are the basis of everything we now know about what she called "the home life of the Chimney Swift."
Courtesy Oberlin College Archives, Oberlin, Ohio

Department of Biological Sciences from 1937 to 1982. His numerous papers explored the relationships among individual birds over many years. Dexter relied primarily on capturing and banding the swifts but also made direct observations. His work was so closely identified with Kent State that the university seal now bears the image of a Chimney Swift.

Richard Fischer was able to confirm many of Sherman's and Dexter's observations in a different setting. He recorded detailed observations of Chimney Swifts nesting not in chimneys or air shafts but on the inside walls of rural farm buildings in New

York State. By studying the birds for fourteen summers from blinds he constructed inside the buildings, Fischer was able to witness the complete breeding and nesting cycles of these secretive birds. He also took some remarkable photographs of swift families on and around the nests at his study sites. His 1958 doctoral dissertation, *The Breeding Biology of the Chimney Swift,* remains one of the most comprehensive published studies of Chimney Swifts.

Margaret Whittemore observed Chimney Swifts for most of her life and hand-reared several orphaned swifts. Through her personal contact with the young swifts, she developed an insight into the "personalities" of individual birds. Her 1981 book, *Chimney Swifts and Their Relatives,* summarized

David Lack, *left,* and Richard Fischer, *right,* investigating a chimney at Cornell University, Ithaca, New York. Fischer studied Chimney Swifts for fourteen years in upstate New York; Lack studied Common Swifts in Europe.
Courtesy Richard B. Fischer

Ralph Dexter with a banded Chimney Swift.
Courtesy Kent State University, Department of Special Collections Archives, Kent, Ohio

Chimney Swift, 1950.
Photo Courtesy Richard B. Fischer

the work of those researchers who preceded her and helped start us on our own path of Chimney Swift research.

The notable works of Sherman, Dexter, Fischer, Whittemore, and others intrigued and fascinated us. However, it was Althea Sherman and her "Chimney Swifts' tower" that most captured our imagination. In 1989, we constructed two wooden Chimney Swift towers of our own and made them an integral part of our home. Because of the design of these towers and video technology not available to our predecessors, we were able to witness the construction of twenty-seven nests, seven second broods, and 115 Chimney Swifts fledging.

View from the nest tower camera.

A nest camera provided a close-up view of the activities in and around the nest. Once the young were old enough to venture from the security of their nest, the overhead camera became more useful. The overhead view was also helpful in studying the activity of a roosting flock. Those observations allowed us to confirm most of what we had read about the birds. In addition, we observed and recorded remarkable behavior that had not previously been formally documented.

During our seventeen years of hand-rearing and rehabilitating injured Chimney Swifts, we banded and released more than eleven hundred of the fifteen hundred individuals that came to us for care.

View from the overhead tower camera.

We purposely banded all hand-reared birds on the right leg and all wild swifts captured in the towers on the left leg. This enabled us to distinguish "our" birds from the rest. In several cases over the years, we have had the remarkably good fortune to have a pair of birds that wore bands on opposite legs take up residence in our observation towers. Because the individuals of the pair were visually distinguishable, we ascertained the gender of each during their mating. This made it possible to study and compare behavior of the male and the female in nest building and in the care of their brood.

Most people—no matter how interested they are—will never be able to personally observe the family life of Chimney Swifts. However, it is our hope that by reporting what we have learned after twenty years and countless hours of observation, we can share the charm and wonder of Chimney Swifts with others.

Social Life of Chimney Swifts in North America

CHIMNEY SWIFTS FOLLOW the warming spring temperatures and emergence of flying insects northward. These "feathered meteors" remain airborne during daylight hours and abandon the sky only when darkness approaches. Swifts roost each night inside chimneys, air shafts, hollow trees, and sites constructed specifically for their use. Communal roosts consisting of a few individuals to thousands of swifts will form inside structures deemed suitable by the birds. Some migrants sneak in for only a night's stay at the equivalent of an avian bed-and-breakfast before continuing their journey home. Other occupants are summer residents, birds that have bred or were hatched in the area in past years and whose northward journey has ended. In any spring roost, swift numbers fluctuate as travelers mingle with resident birds.

Chimney Swifts maintain a very strong bond to their nest site. Mated swifts will usually return to the same nesting shafts faithfully year after year. If one adult fails to return, the survivor courts a new mate and continues to occupy the site. Offspring also return to their area of origin. They will secure mates and nest in close proximity to their parents if suitable structures are available.

Courtship

Pair bonding is apparent soon after the swifts return to their nesting sites. After observing the
dedication that is displayed between mated Chimney Swifts for so many years, we find it easy to
imagine that the bond between mated swifts is held
year-round and that their display each spring simply renews the commitment. Aerial courtship is
depicted as synchronous flying—one bird behind
the other. The birds fly at an ever-increasing speed,
each gravity-defying twist and turn matched iden-
tically and instantaneously. These maneuvers are
punctuated by the birds' exuberant chattering vocalizations. The two swifts careen through the
sky—zigging and zagging like a rabbit being chased
by a fox, only faster and with the added dimen-
sion of altitude changes thrown in for good measure. After these manic maneuvers, the pair will
slow to a graceful glide; the trailing bird will snap
its wings up into a "V" position while continuing
to soar. The bond is secured when the leading bird
responds with a matching "V" as they sail on, chattering excitedly to each other. By marking some
birds and then carefully observing the birds in
flight, Richard Fischer was able to ascertain that
the lead bird is usually a female.

Additional swifts may join in the chase. Three
birds flying may indicate a rivalry for a mate or
may signify in-flight training for a younger bird in
the finer arts of courtship. As many as a dozen
birds occasionally jet across the sky, each behind
the other, resembling a multisectional Japanese
kite. Inevitably, the speed will increase to such a
frenetic pace that individuals veer from the formation as if thrown from the tail of a "crack-the-
whip" game, leaving only the most committed
birds to the pursuit and only the mated pair to "V."

**The courtship "V."
The most distinctive and recognizable flight maneuver of Chimney Swifts is the synchronized "V" of a mated pair.**

Back at the nest site, the betrothed pair contin-ues their courtship in a calmer, more intimate fash-ion. They roost side by side. They will occasion-ally touch bill to bill and gently "fence" with each other. Both birds preen each other's heads with the recipient of the favor closing its eyes and leaning toward its mate. At rest, one bird will often cover its partner's back with a wing: a swift embrace.

Once the pair bond is secure, mated swifts be-gin to actively defend their nest site. Only one pair of swifts will construct a nest in any chimney, no matter how large the structure may be. The resi-dents will display their displeasure toward an in-truding bird by snapping their wings. This is ac-complished by the bird grasping the wall of the chimney with its feet and extending its legs as far as possible, thus pushing the body away from the

A swift embrace.
At rest in the nest site,
a Chimney Swift will often
cover its mate's back
with a wing.

wall. Both wings are brought up slowly and stiffly over its back. Then the bird pushes off from the wall with its feet and claps the wings together as it falls to a lower position on the wall. This maneuver has been dubbed "wing clapping" by some researchers and compared to the sound of a distant clap of thunder by others. It is often preceded by a very sharp repetitive "ticking" call. The wing clap is usually followed by an excited burst of chippering. Both resident birds may join in the activity. If the bold intruder fails to respond to this obvious expression of displeasure, one of the defenders may physically remove the unwelcome visitor. A defending bird will fly toward the roosting interloper, use its feet to grab the interloper's back or wings, and then fly backward, literally pulling the intruder from the wall. Occasionally, both will fall to the floor and engage in a brief wrestling match. Eventually, one bird surrenders and exits the chimney (presumably the intruder) with the other bird in close pursuit.

Some suitable nesting chimneys also house overnight roosting swifts throughout the summer. The phenomenon of summer roosts has become quite common. Long after migrating birds have dispersed to their breeding areas, nocturnal roosts continue. Because each pair of breeding birds remains in its individual chimney at night, the congregations of swifts that are found in summer roosts are probably birds that were unable to locate a mate or nesting site of their own. Consequently, breeding birds nesting in a chimney that also maintains an overnight roost must develop an understanding with their cohorts. The pair will initially attempt a defense of its home, but that becomes impractical when twenty to one hundred birds share the accommodations. Stratification develops that allows the breeding birds to construct a nest in the preferred nesting area by occupying the lower third of the chimney. The roosting birds congregate initially at about the middle section and may move higher as the nest is completed and eggs are deposited. Only one nest is constructed in any shaft, regardless of the number of occupants.

Nest Building

Once clear title to a nesting site has been secured, the devoted mates begin focusing on the construction of a nest. The salivary glands of breeding swifts become enlarged. Close inspection of the inside of the mouth of a breeding swift will reveal swollen tissue under the tongue, and the throat will be slightly distended; the bird appears to have the mumps. The enlarged glands produce copious amounts of saliva. The birds use this glutinous substance as a glue to fasten sticks to the vertical surface of their nesting wall.

Chimney Swifts collect all of their nesting material as they fly. An individual approaches the desired dead tree twig, pine needle, juniper branch, or any locally available brittle vegetation; pauses briefly to grasp the material with its feet; and then flies on. If the bird is successful, the desired construction material will break from the plant on the first try. If not, another attempt will be made. As soon as the building material is secured, the bird transfers the prize to its bill, leaving its feet free to grasp the chimney wall, and returns to the nest site. Upon arriving at the chimney, a decision must be made: where to build the nest?

A spot is selected, and the bird pushes saliva from its mouth onto the wall with its tongue while continuing to hold the stick in its bill. The stick is then placed on the saliva patch, and the bird adds more saliva to the stick and the wall—literally gluing the stick in place. Once dry, the bond is very durable, vulnerable only to heavy rainfall or to peeling loose from a fireplace chimney if a layer of soot has been allowed to accumulate on the wall's surface. The builder's mate will return with a stick and repeat the same process. If the location of the first glued stick is acceptable, the second stick will be placed next to it. If, however, the original spot is deemed inappropriate, the second bird will choose a new location to adhere a stick. The pair continues to place these "test" sticks on the walls until both birds finally concur on a location. With their efforts now focused, they begin to form a nest. Stick by stick, both birds contribute to construction. Each of the pair may have its own idea about what constitutes a "good" stick. In the case of one pair we observed, the female always brought the largest pieces, and the male brought such tiny twigs that they were sometimes indiscernible. Nevertheless, there seemed to be a place in the construction

Swift with a nest stick. Nest sticks are collected with the feet, but they must be transferred to the bill before a swift enters the nest shaft.

for every item—twig or timber—that was gathered.

As their structure grows away from the vertical surface of the wall, the birds apply saliva to preglued sticks in a brick-and-mortar fashion. The saliva does not solidify immediately and may remain pliable for an hour or more. Once a new stick is in place, the swift may tug on other nest sticks to test their durability. The adult will then settle onto the structure, check for a good fit, and may reposition the newly affixed stick. Although the exterior of the nest appears untidy with many protruding sticks, the interior has the qualities of a finely woven basket. A pair will collect and glue between eight and twelve sticks per day. In approximately seven days, the receptacle will accommodate an egg. Even though the nest is far from complete at the time, the female lays an egg.

Mating and Egg Laying

Several days after they choose a nest site, the pair begins to copulate daily. Because Chimney Swifts perform the tasks of eating, drinking, bathing, and collecting nesting material while in flight, it was generally assumed that mating occurred on the wing as well. Richard Fischer was the first to document Chimney Swift copulation. While inside one of his research buildings in 1952, he witnessed and described their terrestrial couplings.

We have also observed and recorded multiple matings via surveillance camera in our observation towers. In our observations, both birds cling to the wall of the nesting structure approximately six inches below the nest location. The male drops below the female and then climbs the wall to position himself beside her with his head even with

Mating usually takes place in the nest site just below the nest.

her back. She preens her breast and shoulders and then pauses. He grasps her rump with a foot, turns toward her, closes his eyes and—amid much fluttering and excited chippering—consummates his objective. The male then flies backward away from the wall and up to the nest, where he clings and preens excitedly as his mate preens on the wall below. Although some species of swifts actually do mate in flight, this seems unlikely with Chimney Swifts, considering the ritual that is involved. On several occasions, we have observed birds coming together in midair and even tumbling to the ground while still clinging to one another. In our opinion, this has appeared to be aggressive behavior rather than mating.

As nest construction and mating continue, an egg will normally be laid every other day until a clutch of two to seven eggs is complete. Newly laid eggs are slightly translucent with a pale pinkish cast, but after a couple of days they will turn pure white. The actual egg laying remained unobserved until 2001. With the aid of a small surveillance camera, we were able to witness a swift laying an egg. Just before dawn, the female climbed from the nest onto the wall just above it and embedded her spiny tail into the stick cradle below her. She began to fluff her feathers until she appeared to be almost twice her normal size—literally filling the nest. She held this position and rocked her head slowly from side to side for the thirty to forty seconds required to expel her egg, which weighed nearly a tenth of her own body weight. She then returned to her normal size and position on the nest. The seemingly anxious male remained attentive to his mate throughout the process. At dawn, they exited the structure together, uttering a continuous cadence of exaggerated chippering. We have since had the opportunity to witness the event on several occasions, and the behavior has always been the same.

The parents exit their nest site but will soon return with additional sticks to bolster the nest. Caution is exercised to prevent the newly laid egg from being dislodged from the nest as construction continues. Slowly and deliberately, a swift will position its body between the egg and the edge of the rudimentary nest before beginning to exude saliva from its mouth. This is a precarious period for any egg in a swift nest. Even the most cautious adult may misjudge a movement and inadvertently send the precious package over the rim. Such accidents are always followed by a period of agitation and intense vocalization from the distraught parents.

Incubation of the Eggs

Incubation of the clutch of eggs usually begins as soon as the next-to-last egg is laid. Both birds share the duties. However, the female tends to spend less time away from the nest during her incubation respites. The relief parent will enter the chimney, land below the nest, and chipper a greeting. The incubating bird responds with a chipper and either flies off the nest or waits until the mate climbs up the wall and onto the nest. Occasionally, they will both remain on the eggs. In cold or rainy weather, both adults will incubate together for extended periods of time during the day and at night. Before a bird exits the structure, it will again chipper, usually receiving a farewell response from the mate. The attending bird will then turn the eggs. The adult holds on to the nest, places its bill on the far side of an egg, and then gently pulls its bill toward its breast, allowing the egg to roll a partial turn. The bird straddles the eggs with chin pressed against the wall and lowers itself onto the eggs

Egg laying.

while rocking from side to side until in total contact with the clutch. Incubation will then continue. The position does not appear to be very comfortable from a human point of view, but it is apparently ideal for Chimney Swifts. More often than not, the bird will close its eyes for a quick nap. It seems astounding that these constantly active individuals surrender so passively to nesting duties.

Throughout the eighteen to twenty-one days of incubation, the swift pair will continue to add sticks to their nest. A returning stick-bearing bird will replace its mate on the nest with the same greeting and response ritual performed at all exchanges. Once the stick is glued in place, the swift settles in to incubate. Because the salivary glands continue to produce saliva, the birds frequently

Eggs in a nest.
Chimney Swifts will lay
as many as seven white
eggs in their meticulously
constructed nest.

Incubation posture.
The position of an
incubating adult may look
uncomfortable. However,
with its chin on the wall,
the attending parent can
easily watch the open sky
at the top of the nest shaft.

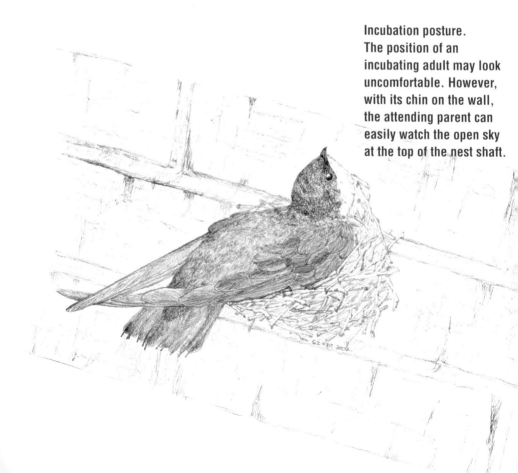

Salivary arch.

find themselves with a mouthful of extra spit. They may add additional layers of "glue" to the edges of the nest where it makes contact with the wall, or they may form a salivary arch on the wall above the nest. Beginning at an edge of the nest, the bird will push saliva from its bill in a continuous curving line until the volume has been completely depleted. Both birds add to this reinforcing arch as they incubate. Sticks may be placed there as well. Some artfully augmented nests take on the appearance of a half basket—complete with a nifty handle.

Emergence of the Hatchlings and Their Care

Around the nineteenth day after incubation was begun, the attending bird (usually the female) will become anxious and agitated. She will stare at the eggs beneath her, fly to the wall below the nest and probe the underside, climb back onto the eggs, touch them with her bill, and briefly settle into the incubating positon before repeating her manic inspection. A baby swift is emerging. The attentive parent apparently detects the sounds of motion and reacts in anticipation of the change that is occurring.

Using its egg tooth, a hatchling swift breaks through its protective shell by piercing a line around the inside circumference of the egg about one-third the distance from the broadest end. This sharp protuberance near the tip of the upper bill provides a handy tool for the hatchling to use to escape from its primitive home. The new baby is no larger than a pink jellybean. Weighing only slightly more than 1.5 grams (about the same as three paper clips), it is totally naked, blind, and little more than mouth, stomach, and feet—very impressive feet. Even when just out of the egg, swifts have a tenacious grip and maintain a firm hold on the sticks of their nest.

After the excitement of the hatching, the female quickly regains her composure and begins to brood her new charge. However, she frequently leans back to make inspections of the new life below her. The empty eggshell halves may remain in the nest for a period of time after the hatchling has emerged. An adult will eventually pick up each half with its bill and, with a flick of the head, toss the remnant over its shoulder to fall to the bottom of the nest shaft.

The return of the off-duty mate to the chimney marks an intense transition for the swift pair. If the bird is carrying a stick, it will be the last one affixed to the nest. From this point on, the devoted parents are committed to the collection and delivery of an abundance of flying insects to feed their new embryonic hatchling.

As the adults exchange places, their movements rouse the exhausted baby. It labors to raise its head on a proportionally long neck, opens a tiny mouth, and utters nearly inaudible peeps. The returning

A four-day-old hatchling. Young Chimney Swifts have very impressive feet. These oversized "grappling hooks" are necessary to keep them safely in their precarious stick cradles.

adult has nothing to offer and settles onto the hatchling and remaining eggs as the other adult exits the nest site to hunt for food. The brooding adult frequently attends the baby and often glances expectantly skyward. As soon as the returning mate chippers its arrival greeting and approaches, the sitting adult relinquishes the nest and chippers on its way out to forage.

Adult swifts capture insects as they fly. Their exceptional eyesight and quick maneuverability allow them to collect a variety of airborne food items. Their preferred prey is seldom more than 0.2 inch long and includes gnats, mosquitoes, flies, winged ants, and termites: all species we as humans prefer to have less of in our immediate environment. Chimney Swifts are very opportunistic and will readily collect an abundance of any small airborne insects that are flying from a mere two feet above ground to hundreds of feet in the air.

Following a thunderstorm, winged ants and termites often emerge from their subterranean abodes on nuptial flights. The steady upward drafts of slow-moving prey provide a banquet for aerial feeders. Chimney Swift parents take full advantage of the resulting bounty. Their collection of the prey and the delivery to their nestlings is exceptionally efficient. On several occasions, we have observed parents feeding nestlings at intervals of five to seven minutes, stuffing insects into the babies' mouths until the young could not close their bills, and insect wings and feet protruded from their mouths. However, a major drawback of thunderstorms is that heavy rainfall can saturate the stick-and-saliva nest, transforming it into a sagging heap that can funnel eggs over the edge or cause the entire nest to peel from a soot-covered chimney wall.

Feeding swifts usually approach their prey from below. They spread their tails at the last instant to slow their speed, raise their heads, and rise to snatch the insect from the air. While collecting meals for the hatchling, a parent will accumulate and hold the prey in its mouth, forming a slurry of body parts and saliva. When satisfied with the catch, the swift returns home. Dropping tailfirst into the chimney and falling past the mate brooding on the nest, it alights on the wall below. Twittering a greeting, it scales the wall to the edge of the nest. The brooding mate chippers in response and leans away from the wall, revealing the hatchling and remaining eggs; the sitting bird then exits. Clinging to the edge of the nest, the returning parent probes among the eggs, closes its eyes, and then prods the hatchling. The baby responds with open bill and outstretched nubs of wings. It takes a moment to make contact, but when hatchling mouth encounters adult bill, the baby latches on. The adult pushes a small amount of the

Feeding in flight. Chimney Swifts feed on small flying insects, including gnats, mosquitoes, flies, winged ants, and termites.

insect mash directly into the hatchling's mouth. As the baby smacks down a mouthful of food, the adult throws its own head back and gulps down the remaining hard-won prey. The satiated baby falls asleep among its eggshell-encased siblings. The adult turns the eggs and resumes brooding duties.

The parents exchange activities of brooding, foraging, and feeding throughout the day while the visiting neighborhood swifts chatter their congratulations as they sail past the chimney. Chimney Swifts socialize with each other throughout the summer. Groups feed together, skim lakes and rivers for water together, and race in the breeze on a windy day. They also fly over each other's nest chimneys and peer inside. As long as no individual

Feeding a hatchling.

commits the faux pas of actually entering an occupied chimney, the swifts are cordial to each
other. The daily "tours" of the neighborhood keep
the members of the swift community apprised of
one another's activities. When a new egg or
hatchling is spotted in any nest by a low-flying
swift, an excited chippering announces the special
occasion. Birds will fly slowly by a chimney; some
will stall over the opening to catch a peek of the
new addition in the nest below. It seems that every Chimney Swift in the area is aware of each new
hatchling. We have repeatedly seen the attending
parent respond to the chippering of other swifts
flying over the nest site by leaning back as if to
expose the hatchlings for the visitors to see. We
have often been awakened early in the morning

by unusually boisterous groups of swifts as they strafe the observation towers on our house. On these mornings, we almost always find that a new egg has been laid or a new hatchling has emerged in one of the towers.

Remaining eggs hatch about eight hours apart and often elicit the same anxious response by the adults as the first hatchling did. Each returning adult feeds all of the babies that react to gentle probing. After a hatchling receives a mouthful of food, the adult throws its bill upward and pulls any protruding food back into its mouth. The process is repeated for the next begging baby swift. The adult then swallows the remainder of the food and performs nest maintenance. A Chimney Swift nest is kept immaculate by the attentive parents. Any fecal material deposited by the hatchlings is picked up and swallowed, eggshells are tossed over the edge, and unhatched eggs are turned. Then the swifts are back to chin-on-the-wall brooding interrupted frequently by preening and baby nuzzling.

There are circumstances that can result in a wide disparity of hatchling ages. Inclement weather may delay the timing of egg laying, or intermediate eggs may be lost over the edge of the nest or fail to hatch. In large clutches of eggs, there may be a span of forty-eight hours or more between the oldest and youngest nest mate. With many avian species, only the strongest (and usually the oldest) nestlings survive. Sibling rivalry resulting in the oldest and largest receiving a disproportionate share of the food often dooms the hapless youngest hatchling to be little more than an insurance policy against the oldest failing to thrive. This is definitely not the case with Chimney Swifts. Zealous swift parents offer food to each hatchling at every exchange. The average feeding interval is thirty minutes. Time and again we have watched in amazement as raucous, well-fed older nest mates are passed over as an adult searches out and feeds the youngest hatchling first. Swifts seem implicitly dedicated to all of their progeny.

Gray dots become apparent under the nestlings' pink skin three days after hatching. These appear in lines along their backs and on the trailing edges of their wings. The dots are feather tracts where the first feather shafts will emerge from under the skin. The hatchlings grow quickly and gain about one gram of weight each day. They sleep in a little pile at the center of the nest with bottoms pointing outward and heads lying over sibling necks like pickup sticks. Frequently, the youngest is relegated

Hatchlings in a nest. Eggs hatch about eight hours apart.

to the bottom of the heap. Chimney Swifts at any age are in almost constant motion. Hatchlings preen long before they have any real feathers, they stretch, they flap, they yawn, they back away from their nest mates to defecate, and they do what all babies do—they wiggle. An adult that is brooding a nest full of hatchlings appears to be atop a popcorn popper.

Care and Development of Nestlings

Five-day-old Chimney Swifts have pinfeathers beginning to protrude from their heads and bodies, and sheath-encased primary feathers are growing from their wings. The adults continue to divide the insects they catch among any nestlings that respond to the offering. This practice changes as the nestlings reach one week of age. The adults will then start feeding only one offspring at a time. The parent will form a ball of insects in its mouth and feed the entire bolus to one individual. All of the nestlings begin their begging calls whenever a parent enters the chimney. Their voices become

Nestling Chimney Swifts. If large clutches of eggs are laid, there may be a span of several days between the oldest and youngest nest mates.

stronger as they grow and begin to compete with each other for food. Their vocalization changes from high-pitched peeps to a rapid, raspy yipping sound. The attentive parents continue to rotate their feeding among all of the nestlings—usually satisfying each over the period of an hour. Brooding diminishes when the parents must devote increasing amounts of time to the collection of flying insects for their voracious young. However, they both pause frequently on the nest after feeding to settle onto the contented nestlings, who squeak and cluck. At night, the parents discontinue feeding their young and roost side by side just below the nest.

Quite often, in a nest full of unbrooded, slumbering Chimney Swifts, one individual will begin to "sing," a phenomenon that Margaret Whittemore reported to her skeptical associates. In an uncharacteristically quiet voice, the nestling utters soft, single notes at metronomic intervals, producing a monotonous "me...me...me...me...me." The nestling occasionally pauses briefly to take a breath or swallow. This mesmerizing lullaby apparently provides a calming influence, because even the "singer" appears to be fast asleep. It is curious that we have never heard more than one nestling sing at a time. We suspect that the singer in any brood is always the same individual but have not been able to positively confirm our suspicions.

When nestlings are one week old, they no longer defecate in the nest. Rather, they back up to the edge of the nest until their abdomen extends slightly over the precipice and then relieve themselves. Their hooklike claws maintain a secure hold on the sticks of the nest as they pull back from the edge and then scuttle back into the security of the pile of their nest mates. Siblings may take exception to being pushed aside by the scrambling

Prickly nestlings. When young Chimney Swifts reach ten days of age, they look rather like prickly lizards or surreal miniature porcupines with silvery quills.

nestling, expressing their displeasure with vocal scolding. Although this sound is similar to the whirring of a child's windup toy, it can also be compared to the warning rattle of a rattlesnake. Richard Fischer described the sound as "raah-raah-raah." Young Chimney Swifts will scold when alarmed—whether the threat is real or imagined. When one begins to scold, all the nest mates soon join in. They will continue their alarm call until—as if by cue—they all abruptly stop. This unique vocalization is discarded once the nestlings have fledged.

During the transition from multiple feedings to single bolus feeding of the nestlings, some parents may become tolerant of additional swifts in the chimney. The nonbreeding attendant birds are often swifts born in the chimney the previous year. Year-old swifts can and do successfully breed, and it is unclear why so many do not. These "helper" birds deliver food to the nestlings and roost with the family at night. One assistant is common at a nest; however, as many as four additional birds may be in attendance.

By the time young Chimney Swifts reach ten days of age, they look rather like prickly lizards or surreal miniature porcupines with silvery quills. All of their practice preening will now be put to good use as their feathers are finally beginning to break through the tips of the feather sheaths. Using the tips of their bills, the birds work the ends of the feather shafts to break the cellophane-like cover. As fragments of the sheath are broken loose, they float and shimmer delicately in the chimney. The tips of the primary wing feathers are the first feathers to unfurl, providing a glossy black contrast to the silvery nestling.

Over the next three or four days, preening nest-

"Frosty-faced" nestlings. Remnants of silvery feather sheath remain around the faces and heads of twenty-one-day-old nestlings, giving them a frosty-faced appearance.

lings transform into softly feathered birds. Their stubby wings, short spiny tail, and plump body have now turned black. The few remnants of silvery feather sheath around the face and head give the birds a "frosty-faced" appearance. Four or five fluffy nestlings will now completely obscure the stick cradle to which they still cling.

During this time, the nestlings will begin to open their eyes. The process seems difficult for the young swifts, who will initially be able only to crack one eye open. At first, their eyes are a milky blue color, the lids are wrinkled, and the birds appear to have difficulty focusing. However, they have no difficulty continuing to react to their parents returning with food offerings. The sound of an adult's wings as it enters the chimney or the parents' vocal greeting elicits an ever-growing raucous response from the nestlings. Even though the nestlings are now feathered and able to regulate their own body temperature, their doting parents will continue to climb onto the nest, making close contact by covering their babies with wings and body.

Human Interference

Until this point in the young swifts' development, the co-owners of the chimney (the human occupants of the structure attached) have paid little attention to the activities occurring only feet away from their daily activities. They may have occasionally heard a chippering or a strange clapping sound. The family cat or dog may be spending time in front of the fireplace with head cocked, but this draws little response from its owners. There is a point, however, at which the volume and pitch of the exuberant begging call of the young swifts breeches the threshold of human hearing. To many, the sound is not pleasant. Homeowners unaware of the drama unfolding within their fireplace chimney may take uninformed actions to rid their home of the bizarre sounds. Small fires are built in an attempt to evict the noisemakers. This produces toxic smoke, which causes immediate and irreparable damage to the delicate respiratory system of the nestlings. Incapable of flight and unable to escape, the normally resilient babies will slowly die in their nest over a period of several hours or even days. Some may tumble from the nest in a panic and actually fall into the flames. An adult attending the nestlings at the time of the catastrophe will not abandon them and will suffer the same fate as its young. A returning adult will attempt to rouse the dead or dying nestlings, to no avail, but will remain with them.

Other homeowners may call a chimney-cleaning company to help determine the source of the unearthly noise. Disreputable or uninformed chimney sweeps may illegally scrape the nest, with young attached, from the chimney wall or vacuum the babies from their home before installing a cap on the chimney. Returning adult swifts find an impenetrable barrier to their home. They will dive repeatedly at the chimney cap, searching unsuccessfully for a point of entry. Eventually, they abandon the futile attempt and begin to search for an alternative nesting site. The search is usually unproductive because most available chimneys have been claimed by other breeding pairs. The displaced parents will be relegated to spending their nights in the upper region of a communal roost.

Chimney Swifts, their nests, their eggs, and their young are protected under the Migratory Bird Treaty Act of 1916. However, even if inhumane interventions were not a violation of federal law, the cruelty of such actions would be difficult to justify. There are humane alternatives to the unlawful destruction of nesting Chimney Swifts.

Fortunately for many Chimney Swifts, most human landlords pursue a more informed course of action. Referring to the birds as "chimney sweets" and describing the begging calls as the sound of "elves laughing in the woods," some homeowners delight in hearing the boisterous calls of the nestlings. "Gim-me, gim-me, gim-me" is one translation by a devotee fully aware that swift parents are offering the noisemakers hundreds of flying insect pests at every outburst. Most first-time swift landlords investigate the inhabitants of the chimney before taking any unwarranted action. Professional chimney sweeps are becoming more aware of the beneficial nature of Chimney Swifts

Adult with nestlings.

and respect the laws intended to protect the birds. A consultation with their clients about the birds and a rescheduled service call after the young have fledged are usually all that are needed to calm any fears or uncertainties about having Chimney Swifts nesting in their chimney. Hopefully, the newly educated homeowner will tolerate the swifts that currently inhabit their chimney and will welcome the return of the swifts in the seasons to come.

From the Nest to the Wall

Those nestlings that are not molested will prosper in their secure home. They are finally able to focus their bright eyes (now brown in color) and are feeling cramped on the nest. They now weigh as much as or more than their parents, and their body is the size of an adult's. Their tails are still growing, as are their wings, which hang to their sides barely longer than their plump torsos.

In many ways, nestling Chimney Swifts' early behavior is similar to that of songbirds. However, as soon as their eyes open and their feathers unfurl, young Chimney Swifts become completely unique. The oldest nestling will be the first to venture from the horizontal lifestyle. From our point of view, as incurable observers, this is probably the most charming (and often humorous) stage of the Chimney Swifts' development. We will now follow the adventures of a representative individual as "he" gets vertical.

As a first step, he grasps the wall above the nest with one foot and—as a mountain climber does—tests his footing before taking another step up. There he will cling, with his tail in the nest, and inspect his surroundings from this new perspective. He will preen and nap but usually will return to the nest when a parent enters with food.

Our young swift is a curious little imp, and he will soon begin to explore the few square feet around the nest. Again, each step taken is deliberate and well tested before the other foot is moved. Swifts of all ages require the aid of their wings when traversing vertical surfaces on foot, and both wings flutter as the birds ascend a wall, providing momentum and lift for every step. On descent, birds that are capable of flight simply push off the wall and allow gravity to propel them downward tailfirst as they extend their wings and flap to maintain equilibrium or slow their speed. Our young swift would fall like a rock if he attempted such a maneuver. An alternative method of backtracking must be employed. As a child discovers on climbing a tree for the first time, the swift finds that going up is far easier than coming back down. He peers over his shoulder at his siblings secure on the nest below. He raises his wings and flaps as he tentatively releases his grip on the wall with one foot and reaches for a secure hold slightly lower— but there is a "spiny-tail problem." As the bird ventures upward, the tail spines support his body weight and act as a braking system that ratchets upward with each forward step. Stepping downward forces the tail bristles propped on the wall to pivot out at a greater angle, scrunching the nestling into an inchworm-like posture. The swift pauses. After a brief problem-solving interval, he steps back up to his starting position and then repeats the step downward while simultaneously lifting his tail. Mission accomplished. The young explorer can now move downward almost as effortlessly as upward.

Each nestling will practice the transition from horizontal to vertical lifestyle throughout the day but will never venture far from the security of the nest. Even siblings whose eyes have yet to open may

leave the nest to maintain seemingly critical physical contact with their adventurous older nest mates.

Learning to Fly

While on the nest or on the wall, the nestlings
spend ample time preening their feathers and
stretching their wings. Occasionally, their wings
seem to take on a life of their own as they flick out
from the birds' sides. Double-checking his firm grip
on the wall, our three-week-old swift will lean
back—using his tail for support—and begin to flap
his wings. Initially, he lazily beats out a slow cadence, frequently pausing with both wings outstretched. After the warm-up, he will determinedly
flap as rapidly as possible until he is breathless.
Siblings that are alongside receive a considerable
beating throughout the process—but seldom complain.

Sometimes accidents do happen, and a young
swift will lose its footing and fall to the bottom of
the nest shaft. As long as it can grab hold of the
wall, it will usually be able to work its way back
up to the other nestlings. Although the parents
cannot physically return their wayward offspring
to the nest, they will often fly down to roost next
to the young swift and give encouragement. By
inching up the wall just above the baby, in most
cases a parent is able to coax a fallen youngster
back up the wall by slowly leading the way.

Parents continue to shuttle insects to their offspring, and the activity seems to be taking a toll.
The always ravenous and now mobile nestlings
clamor for attention as they scurry toward the returning adult. The youngster nearest the parent
will grab the food-bearing bill with its own mouth
and begin to gulp—nearly swallowing the adult's
face. We know from our own hand-rearing expe-

rience that the amount of suction exerted by a young swift is considerable. The parents always close their eyes in a protective response when approaching their young; however, their faces are routinely slathered during the feeding process. Clinging beside the satiated youngster, the eyes-closed adult will swallow and appear to doze briefly before jolting awake, chippering, and flying quickly out of the chimney to secure another mouthful of flying insects.

While awaiting their next meal, the nestlings resume their adventures. They master climbing on and off the nest and traveling side to side, as well as up and down, on the chimney wall. A corner poses a new challenge for the swift's intellect, but soon all four chimney walls will be explored. We once observed an individual approach a corner in one of its first explorations. When it was unable

Feeding a fledgling.

to extend both wings equally due to the confines, it seemed baffled. It would stare at the offending wall, lean away, and try again. Finally, the puzzled fledgling raised both wings, reached out a foot, grabbed the new wall, and completed its corner traverse.

Young swifts will begin using a new vocalization during this developmental period. The perky youngsters will utter a quiet and engaging "pee-dah, pee-dah, pee-dah" before changing their position on the wall. They seem to be sharing their secret about the next move that they plan to make.

The adults persist in landing just below the nest as they return with insect offerings; consequently, wandering babies are not fed. Hunger overcomes curiosity, compelling the youngsters to return to the nest area. Within a day or two of the first big adventure away from the nest, the young swifts will normally abandon their nest and begin to roost beneath it with their parents at night.

Early in the season, mated Chimney Swifts will construct a new nest if the first is dislodged from the wall and produce additional eggs if the first clutch fails. Experienced mates that have successfully reared a brood to the stage of having their young roosting below the nest may attempt to raise a second brood. As soon as the nest is vacated, the pair begins copulating between feeding forays and making repairs to the nest by adding more sticks and saliva. Eggs will again be deposited every other day. Incubation activity will not commence until the next-to-last egg is laid, allowing the parents time to devote to the final fledging stage of the first brood.

"Practice flapping" becomes contagious among the siblings. To avoid wing interference, they begin to move away from each other on the chimney wall. The primary flight feathers continue to grow,

Practice flapping. Young swifts will exercise their wings by tightly gripping the wall or nest and flapping vigorously —often until they are panting and out of breath.

and the oldest fledglings' wings are now long enough to touch each other over their tails. Well-developed pectoral muscles in combination with the increasing wing surface allow our representative swift to produce enough lift when flapping to propel his body away from the wall, leaving only his claws in contact with the surface. While rapidly flapping, he will release his grip and become airborne for the first time. He holds his legs out stiffly, ready to grasp the chimney wall again as he flies backward and falls downward tailfirst. He is in the air only a second or two before he regains a firm hold on the wall. Exhilarated, he will continue to practice flap until exhausted or distracted by an adult entering the chimney with food.

Each day, his skill and confidence increase. Soon he will master the ability to fly upward rather than merely control downward free fall. He will release his grip, fly several feet upward, stall briefly, and then drop back down to grasp the wall. Like a yo-yo on an invisible string, he rises and falls on whirling wings.

Into the Sky

Flight training within the chimney is normally completed by the time the swifts are twenty-eight days old. They have watched their parents fly in and out of the chimney on insect shuttles at intervals of one to forty-eight minutes, every day, from dawn to dusk. The oldest occasionally follows them as they exit, getting closer to the chimney opening each time before hesitating and rejoining his nest mates. Our little guy is cocky and inquisitive when he finally bursts from the confines of the dark chimney shaft.

He encounters bright light, wind, treetop obstacles, a myriad of sights, and a cacophony of sounds unsuspected from inside the confines of the chimney. There is no wall to grasp, and he wavers. A Chimney Swift must fly perfectly on its first flight if it is to survive—there is seldom a second chance for a bird that is unable to perch. He flaps furiously on unsteady wings (unaware of the concept of "glide") as his parents flank him. They slow their speed to match that of their fledgling, and soon all three are flapping and gliding together in wide circles around their chimney home. Additional swifts often join the noisy graduation parade.

The first excursion rarely lasts very long. The parents escort the fledgling back to the chimney, where he may require several approaches before regaining entry. The critical reentry maneuver is a variation on all of the tailfirst falls from the chimney wall.

Tower entry. Chimney Swifts usually drop into a nest or roost site tailfirst with their wings up.

Back inside, he will preen, practice flying up, down, and from wall to wall while waiting with his nest mates for insect boluses from his parents. Depending on the individual, the second flight from the chimney may occur from several hours to an entire day after the initial flight. Each nestling fledges at its own pace and appears to receive the same support and encouragement from the parents as the first did. As their capabilities improve, the fledglings instinctively begin to collect their own flying insects. Dutiful adults continue to feed the fledglings inside the chimney during the transition. We have observed adults enter a tower with a bolus in their throat after their young have all fledged. If after looking around they find the nest site empty, they will swallow the food they have collected.

The full, glossy black wings differentiate the fledglings from the molting adults as they all fly together. Shortly after the arrival to the breeding area in spring, adult swifts begin their yearly molt. The first feathers to be replaced are the primary flight feathers on the birds' wings. A single feather is dropped from each wing simultaneously, beginning with those closest to the bird's body. As soon as the new feathers are partially grown, the subsequent pair of feathers will be molted symmetrically. The process requires months to complete. An obvious notch or "window" on the trailing edge of both wings (as well as the contrast in color of the newly grown feathers compared to that of the year-old worn feathers) provides recognition of adult Chimney Swifts. Family groups can be easily identified as they fly together in noisy parades throughout the day. The fledglings are escorted to local rivers, lakes, and ponds to practice water skimming. They become proficient at collecting flying insects and master the intricate nuances of swift flight and midair preening. The Chimney Swift fledglings are now where they belong: in the relative safety and absolute freedom of the sky.

Fledglings on Patrol

Five-week-old Chimney Swifts are self-feeding and independent and begin to interact with other neighborhood fledglings. Their impish, inquisitive nature prompts sophomoric conduct as they airily explore their world together. A tree rising above the surrounding canopy provides an axis for helical maneuvers. The birds follow each other in circles until a companion swerves aside and re-

Adult wing during molt, *top*, and juvenile wing, *bottom*.

Fledglings on patrol.

enters the foray head-on. They may all reverse course or spiral into multiple directions—banking at the last possible instant to avoid midair collisions. Some will dive under the tree canopy and thread their way through the undergrowth at breakneck speed. They play "follow-the-leader" and grab at a tree twig or leaf, each pausing to tag the totem before flying on.

Other species of birds seem to hold extreme fascination for young swifts. House Finches, Mourning Doves, and especially Northern Cardinals learn quickly to dive for cover when a drag-racing fledgling targets them for play. None are able to outfly the fleet swifts. Hummingbirds are also frequently buzzed. The hummers soon tire of the dive-bombing interruptions and will often engage their swift tormentor. After a fledgling makes a playful pass, the pint-sized, long-billed, whirling dervish of a hummingbird will fly after the swift. The confident fledgling will slow its speed and allow the hummingbird to approach before kicking into overdrive, leaving the exasperated hummingbird behind. We have also been the objects of *Chaetura* curiosity. While we stand on our deck and stare up at the sky watching a group of swifts

Chimney Swift Flight Maneuvers

The flight of Chimney Swifts may seem erratic and random to the casual observer. However, careful observation will reveal Chimney Swift courtship, feeding, and play behavior. Watch for these Chimney Swift maneuvers.

Kiting: Four or more swifts fly in unison as if connected by invisible strings.

Crack-the-Whip: A more "manic" high-speed version of "kiting," where the last birds are unable to negotiate a final turn and break away from the group. These individuals will often take the lead as the group re-forms.

The Chase: Two or more swifts fly in high-speed pursuit of a lead bird—usually a female. There is a lot of wing flapping but not much gliding involved in a chase.

The "V": This position is the usual culmination of a chase—the second bird raises its wings in a stationary "V" position over its back. If the lead bird is responsive to the chaser, the lead bird will respond with the same posture. A "double V" usually indicates a mated pair. In undeniably one of the most graceful of the Chimney Swifts' flight maneuvers, a pair will glide together in gentle, seemingly choreographed movements not unlike those of figure skaters. A duet of vocalizations normally accompanies the activity. A mated pair will continue to "V" with each other throughout their stay in North America.

The Stall and Turn: The wings are held extended, and the tail is spread completely open to slow the swift just before a turn.

The Munch: Coming up from below an insect, a swift will glide and then surge slightly upward with its neck extended and head raised as it captures prey in its mouth. This is usually followed with a quick flutter of the wings and a short glide.

Kiting

The Tumble and Peek: This maneuver is used to investigate a chimney, shaft, or anything of interest to a swift. Spilling air from its wings by holding them up in a "V" position and rocking slightly from side to side with tail spread, a swift will drop quickly and stall slightly before taking off again in a surge of wing flapping. This may be frequently observed over a nest site where a new egg has been laid or where a new hatchling is emerging. Persistent Chimney Swift observers may also find themselves the objects of the "tumble and peek."

The Parade: Shortly after young swifts fledge, they will accompany their parents and other swifts in uncharacteristically slow, noisy, gliding flyovers of the area around the nest site. During this maneuver, it is particularly easy to identify the young birds by their broad, dark, solid wings. The wings of the adults will appear almost ragged by comparison.

The Tag: Young swifts will follow one another, and as their flight abilities improve, they will select a particular spot or object to briefly "tag" with their feet. Each of the birds will tag the same spot in turn and fly off to follow the leader. Resident songbirds are seldom amused when they are sometimes selected as "It."

Dropping In: Some swifts will enter a nest or roost site feetfirst, perfectly positioned to grasp the wall; others may dive in headfirst and pull up just in time to right themselves. Observing the different styles of entry at dusk can be very entertaining.

fly, an individual may tumble within just a few feet of us, pause, and then fly on. Less bold individuals make their approach from behind and pass close enough for us to hear or even feel the wind in their wings as they zip by.

Mated swifts that are free of parental duties often return to their chimney together during the day. They cling side by side beneath the nest and preen together and may even begin a second brood. Pairs that already have a second clutch of eggs resume incubation and will soon have more tiny mouths to fill with insects.

Communal Roosts

Experienced fledglings may remain airborne from dawn to dusk. Some may return to roost with their parents and siblings at night while others visit nearby nest sites or join the social gathering at a local communal roost. Residential chimneys often host relatively small roosts of a dozen or so birds, but most communal roosts are located in large industrial chimneys, stacks, incinerators, or air shafts. The vast majority of these structures were constructed in the late 1800s and early 1900s, and they are no longer used for their original purpose. Chimney Swifts now utilize the available shafts as overnight accommodations.

As dusk approaches, clusters of from two to five Chimney Swifts arrive at the roost site and fly in close association with each other. Pairs of mated swifts often join the social gathering, leaving their eggs and nestlings unattended. Just at sunset, the swifts will leave the area, possibly going for their "sundowner" drink at the nearest body of water. The sky is swift-free only briefly before the birds noisily announce their arrival. Parent swifts return to their nest chimneys to resume brooding and

A roosting cluster. In a roost, swifts appear to shingle the wall, but they do not hold on to each other. Any swift that grabs hold of a neighbor's back is met with vocal complaints and quickly disengages.

atically molted and replaced. Most body feathers have also been replenished. Swifts will hitch a ride on fast-moving cold fronts—stopping each evening at historical roost sites.

As roost sizes diminish in northern areas, swifts' numbers begin to swell along migration routes. Now the spectacular evening roost displays commence. At dusk, swifts arrive and, as always, are heard before they are seen. Individuals and small groups lazily glide into the area from every direction. They crisscross each other's paths as they feed, chase, and "V." A few minutes past the day's official sunset time, the groups form a more cohesive flight pattern and begin to circle above the roost structure. The general direction of flight is in unison, but as additional swifts arrive, the spiral is disrupted. The swifts may reverse course, fly in a figure eight, or disband briefly into a multidirectional swarm. They will regroup and begin to circle again. Now, however, the roost shaft will be below the edge of the circle of swirling birds rather than at the center. Swifts passing over the opening will stall, peer inside, and then flap on, sometimes inadvertently slapping each other's wings. Additional swifts continue to arrive.

Looking straight up at a roost site, we have often seen swifts spiraling at all altitudes, with some appearing as small, black dots just at the limit of eyesight. The noisy throng accelerates in its merry-go-round ritual, making invisible skid marks in the sky before entering their hostel. Some individuals rock from side to side to spill air from their wings, then spread the tail, raise wings, and disappear inside. Others fly in headfirst, barely checking their speed. Not all remain inside; some will pop back out to rejoin the eddy. About twenty minutes past sunset, urgency arises among the swifts. Instead of several individuals entering the roost at every spiraling rotation, they begin to stream in as if a vacuum cleaner were sucking them from the sky. Within five minutes, 70 percent of the nightly occupants may have entered. In roosts containing several hundred swifts per night, the sight is impressive. If a roost consists of several thousand birds, the phenomenon can take your breath away. Swifts will continue to circle and enter while the roosting birds chipper loudly. Often, a single swift will remain in the air after the sky seems otherwise swift-free. The sentinel will circle the structure, pause to peer inside, and then fly wide circuits overhead. Late arrivals will fly directly into the roost, omitting the characteristic circling. The sky becomes darker, and a screech-owl may begin to vocalize as single swifts continue to enter. The sentinel is now just a shadow against the sky, when another swift or two appear and dive into the abyss. Finally, the last swift follows them in— as if roll call were complete. Inside the roost, swifts cling side by side, chipper, and preen. They seem incapable of holding still, and some will fly from wall to wall within the structure throughout the night, impatiently waiting for dawn.

At first light, Chimney Swifts bubble from the tower. They flicker and float in loose association until the throng has assembled. Only the swifts know when it is their time to move on. But when a major cold front is expected to pass through the area, they most certainly will spread their wings and ride the air mass south like surfers on a wave. One day the sky is overflowing with the exuberant calls of the swifts, and the next day it is strangely silent. The Chimney Swifts have gone on vacation. We wish them a safe journey.

Maintaining and Protecting Existing Habitat

Being a Good Chimney Swift Landlord

BECAUSE OF THEIR REMARKABLE adaptability and expansion in range over the last century, Chimney Swifts would seem to be an exception to the generally declining populations of migratory birds. Unfortunately, this is not the case.

There can be little doubt that Chimney Swifts are experiencing difficulties on their breeding grounds in North America. They commonly roost together in large numbers in a single shaft. However, each breeding pair must have a site of its own to raise young. Finding suitable nesting sites has become a problem for the species largely as a result of the increasing desire of homeowners to have their chimneys capped by professional chimney-maintenance companies.

Chimney Swifts are a vital part of an overall healthy North American ecology, and their decrease in numbers is a symptom of a general decline in the quality of life for all species, including our own. However, their conservation is not only possible but relatively simple. Anyone with a masonry chimney can participate. With tolerance, a little education, and proper timing, humans can make a significant contribution to the future well-being of this beneficial and uniquely North American species. Providing nesting sites for Chimney Swifts is not as easy as putting up a prefabricated Purple Martin house or hanging out a nest box for Carolina Wrens, but it can be as simple as properly maintaining an existing fireplace chimney. Because Chimney Swifts are in North America only during the warmest part of the year, there is seldom a conflict over time-sharing rights of a chimney.

For a chimney to be suitable for swifts, the inside must be made of stone, firebrick, or masonry flue tiles with mortared joints. These materials provide enough texture for the birds to be able to cling to the walls. Metal chimneys are unsuitable and should always be capped. Any animal that enters a metal flue will fall to the bottom and be unable to climb the slippery walls.

Proper maintenance is crucial for any chimney, whether it is to be used by Chimney Swifts or for winter fires. Wood fires produce flammable creosote residue that coats the inside of a chimney. If the chimney is left unattended for more than a single season, this material will build up, and the entire layer may ignite with catastrophic results. A resulting chimney fire will spew burning cinders onto the roof and surrounding structures. The intense heat of such a fire may also cause permanent damage to the chimney. In most cases, an annual cleaning will keep the chimney walls clean and safe for swifts and homeowners alike. Most home hardware-supply stores carry chimney-cleaning kits. For those not inclined to be do-it-yourselfers, there are many commercial chimney-cleaning companies that can be hired to handle the annual task.

Chimney Swifts build their nests by attaching small twigs to the chimney wall with their gluelike

An open chimney.
Unlike most avian species
that require expanses of
terrestrial habitat,
Chimney Swifts' habitat
is primarily open sky.
Their conservation
requires only that they are
provided with a place to
roost at night and raise
their young. An excellent
space is an uncapped
masonry chimney.

saliva. When completed, the shallow half-cup nest protrudes two to three inches from the wall. The most common cause of mortality in baby Chimney Swifts is fallen nests. By keeping the chimney free of creosote buildup, homeowners help assure successful nest building and decrease the chances of the nest falling before the birds have fledged. Action should be taken before the swifts return from their wintering grounds in South America. The best time to clean a chimney is in mid-March or when the local wood-fire season is over.

More and more homeowners are electing to have their chimneys capped to prevent water damage and to act as spark arresters when the fireplace is in use during the winter. In fact, some insurance companies require chimney caps be installed as a condition of their coverage. However, it is a simple matter to arrange with your chimney-cleaning professional to have the cap removed in the spring before the swifts arrive. It can then be replaced in the fall in preparation for a safe wood-fire season after the swifts have migrated south. Another option is to install a cover that is open on the sides to shield the chimney from rain but still allow access to the swifts. These covers can actually be attractive as well as functional. As long as there is at least a twelve-inch space between the top of the chimney and the cover, the swifts should have no trouble finding their way into the chimney.

The damper should be inspected during the annual chimney cleaning and should remain closed during the nesting season. This will prevent birds from flying into the house and becoming trapped or injured. A closed damper will also prevent a nest that does break loose from falling into the fireplace. In addition, it lessens the transfer of sound and will make the chimney quieter for the birds and homeowners alike. In older homes, some

A capped chimney. The increasing desire of homeowners to have their chimneys capped by professional chimney-maintenance companies, coupled with the demolition of old buildings and their masonry chimneys, has dramatically diminished the number of suitable nesting sites for Chimney Swifts.

fireplaces may not have dampers, or the dampers may be inoperative. In these cases, a large piece of foam rubber (do not use fiberglass insulation) can be wedged up from the fireplace to serve this purpose while the swifts are in residence. If foam rubber is placed in the flue, it is a good idea to write a note and leave it near the fireplace so that the foam rubber is removed before the first fire of the season is lit in the fall.

Chimney Swifts are protected by federal law under the Migratory Bird Treaty Act. Unfortunately, some chimney-cleaning companies will still illegally remove active nests with young and discard the nestlings to die slowly in trash receptacles. When hiring a professional chimney-cleaning company, be careful to select one that is reputable. There are many companies that now actively promote Chimney Swift conservation. Always keep in mind that "bird removal" is a blatant violation of the state and federal laws that protect Chimney Swifts and other migratory birds. Homeowners should inquire about a company's policy regarding Chimney Swifts. Any company that offers or advertises a bird-removal service should be avoided.

Frequently Asked Questions

Are bats in my chimney?

The environmental conditions in a chimney are just not what bats are looking for. Bats like tight spaces that are open at the bottom and closed at the top. Chimney Swifts like wider spaces that are open on the top and closed on the bottom.

I hear raucous sounds from the chimney. Will they go on forever?

Chimney Swifts create a variety of sounds during their stay in North America during the warmer months. There is the "whooshing" sound of their wings as the swifts come and go from the chimney. They utter a gentle "chippering" as they socialize with one another in the roost during nest building and at night. The most audible sounds are those of the young, which have two basic vocalizations: the very loud, high-pitched, "yippering" feeding call as they beg for food from the returning parents; and their mechanical, hissing alarm call when disturbed or frightened.

As long as the young are making the loud feeding call, they are incapable of sustained flight and are completely dependent on their parents for food. Homeowners' tolerance during this critical period of the swifts' development is very important. If the young are forced from the chimney during this period, they will perish, slowly starving to death over a period of several days. The parents are unable to care for the nestlings outside their chimney. Once the sound of the young becomes noticeable, the birds are usually only fourteen days or so from fledging.

Are Chimney Swifts swallows?

Although there are some striking similarities between swifts and swallows, they are not closely related. Swallows use mud when building their nests, but Chimney Swifts use only sticks and their saliva. Chimney Swifts very rarely build their nests in visible locations as swallows do. Swallows perch, and Chimney Swifts cling to vertical surfaces.

Do Chimney Swifts and Purple Martins interfere with each others' feeding and nesting activities?

Chimney Swifts generally eat smaller insects than Purple Martins do, and their nesting requirements are very different. Many homes with Purple Martin houses in their backyards also have Chimney Swifts in their chimneys, and some Purple Martin landlords now have active Chimney Swift towers as well.

Do Chimney Swifts flap their wings alternately?

Although the illusion is impressive, it has been disproved with the use of stroboscopic photography.

Do Chimney Swifts have small, weak feet?

Because Chimney Swifts have evolved to cling vertically rather than stand, they have difficulty taking off from the ground. Their feet and legs are actually quite strong. When in flight, they tuck their feet and legs so close to their bodies that they do appear to be "without feet." Some species of swifts have feet in which all four toes point forward. However, Chimney Swifts' feet have three toes pointing forward and one toe pointing backward.

Do Chimney Swifts interfere with fireplace usage?

Chimney Swifts are not in North America during the months of November through February, so there is seldom a conflict.

Are Chimney Swift nests a fire hazard?

The nests of Chimney Swifts are small, compact structures that are very unlike the bulky nests of House Sparrows and some other birds. It would be impossible for a Chimney Swift nest to block even the smallest flue. Furthermore, Chimney Swifts nest only during the summer when chimneys are not needed. When a chimney is properly maintained, the old nest is removed after the swifts no longer need it. Chimney Swifts will easily build a new nest every year.

Do Chimney Swifts' wings sweep the chimney clean?

As desirable as it would be, Chimney Swifts cannot and do not clean a dirty chimney. For this, you will need an annual interior cleaning. Whether you do it yourself with a specialized wire brush and vacuum or hire a professional to handle the job, a clean chimney is important for the safety of homeowners and Chimney Swifts alike.

If I place young swifts in a box on the roof will they survive?

Placing young swifts that have fallen into the fireplace in a box on the roof is a certain death sentence. The parents will be unable to land and feed their young unless they are inside the nest chimney.

Will Chimney Swifts infest a chimney with mites?

Like all birds (as well as domestic dogs and cats), Chimney Swifts do have some ecto-parasites that are a natural part of their lives. However, they do not suffer the severe infestations of mites that even the well-loved Purple Martins must endure. Chimney Swift bugs (*Cimexopsis nyctalis*) are specific to the Chimney Swift and do not feed on other organisms. Swifts also have species-specific feather lice (*Dennyus dubius*) that are with them throughout their lives and never leave the swifts' feathers.

Do Chimney Swifts carry diseases that affect people?

In spite of claims by some chimney-cleaning companies, Chimney Swifts do not carry or cause histoplasmosis. *Histoplasma* is an organism that grows in soil that has been associated mainly with large concentrations of poultry. Although it is possible that very large concentrations of the droppings of any animal can present a health concern, an annual chimney cleaning, scheduled so it does not interfere with the breeding activities of the swifts, will prevent any potential problems from arising. In reality, Chimney Swifts provide a valuable service by eating mosquitoes and other flying insect pests, making the swifts an asset to public health.

Are there multiple active nests in the chimney?

Many observers may get the mistaken impression that the presence of many swifts in a single structure indicates that there are multiple nests at the same site. Likewise, an inspection of any site that has not been cleaned of old nests may give the same impression. However, no matter how large a chimney is or how many swifts enter it in the evening to roost, there will be only one active nest in any chimney in any single year. Chimney Swifts are communal roosters, but they are solitary nesters.

Will capping my chimneys make much difference in Chimney Swift habitat?

Every masonry chimney is important: Chimney Swifts will attempt to return to the same chimney year after year. Every chimney that has housed Chimney Swifts in the past that is capped evicts a Chimney Swift family. Just imagine returning from your vacation and finding that the locks on your doors have been changed and there are burglar bars on all of your windows. Where would you go from there?

Coming to the Aid of Adults and Juveniles

ALTHOUGH CHIMNEY SWIFTS LIKE TO inhabit chimneys, it is likely that they never intend to enter living rooms. However, accidents do happen. If a Chimney Swift does manage to slip past the damper and end up in the fireplace, it is important to determine if the bird is an adult or a juvenile. An adult will usually be able to free itself with just a little assistance from the homeowner. An older juvenile may look very similar to an adult but will not be able to survive if improperly handled.

Adults have very long wings that cross noticeably over the tail when the bird is at rest. Adults are also usually silent when trapped and confronted by people. Juvenile swifts' wings are shorter than the body, and the youngsters will be very vocal when approached. They will either complain loudly with their alarm call or make the begging call—expecting to be fed (see "Social Life of Chimney Swifts in North America").

An adult will instinctively attempt to escape the fireplace by flying toward the room—the place where there is the most light. If the bird is contained in the fireplace by glass doors or a fire screen, it can usually be persuaded to fly back up the chimney. To accomplish this, completely cover the front of the fireplace with a dark blanket. Darken the room by closing all shades and drapes, and turn off all lights. The swift will be drawn to the light coming down the chimney and will be able to find its way back out. Once the bird has left, make certain that the area above the fireplace is closed off by the damper or a wedge of foam rubber.

If a swift has not found its way up the chimney after an hour or does manage to find its way into the house, it may need to be hand-captured. To accomplish this, seal off the room where the swift is found. Cover all windows, and darken the room. If possible, open a single door or window that leads to the outside, and the swift will be drawn toward the light.

If it is necessary to hand-capture a Chimney Swift, wait until the bird has come to rest on a vertical surface. Quickly but gently cup a hand over the bird's back—holding it to the surface on which it is clinging. Gently close your hand around the swift by working your fingers between the bird and its roosting surface. The swift will usually take hold of your hand. A Chimney Swift will not bite or scratch when captured, but do not be startled by the strength of its grip. With your free hand, carefully work loose any claws that are still cling-ing to the surface.

If there is any doubt whether a captured swift is a juvenile or an adult, it is best to return it to the chimney rather than release it outside. If a young Chimney Swift is released outside before it is completely mature, it will not survive. The par-ent birds will not be able to find and feed their young anywhere outside the original nest chimney. To replace the bird from below, reach above the damper, and hold the bird against the wall of the chimney until it has a good grasp of the wall. Slowly remove your hand, and then slowly close the damper. To replace a bird from above, reach as far down into the chimney as possible before placing the bird against the inside chimney wall. Hold your hand cupped over the bird until you are certain that it has a firm hold. Then, slowly remove your hand, and back away from the chimney. Do not stay on the roof, because that will frighten the parents and prevent them from entering and caring for their young.

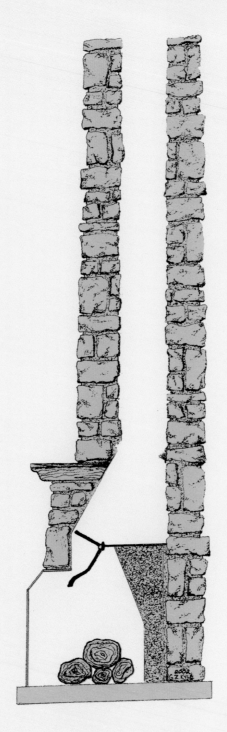

**Diagram of a
typical chimney.**

What to Do with a Fallen Chimney Swift Nest

KEEPING A CHIMNEY CLEAN and the damper closed will eliminate most of the problems that arise between people and Chimney Swifts. However, despite homeowners' best efforts, there will still be occasions when a nest will fall, and very young Chimney Swifts will end up in the fireplace where the parents are unable to care for them. The young may desperately cling to the nest or be found crawling blindly across the living room floor. The homeowners will often respond to these helpless waifs by attempting to feed and care for them. However, wildlife rehabilitators insist that it is always best to reunite wild baby birds with their parents—whatever the species. This is particularly true with Chimney Swifts because of their specific diet and handling and housing requirements.

Chimney Swifts nest in inaccessible places, so returning the young to their parents is an exceptional challenge. If the birds are feathered, they can be placed on the wall above the damper as previously described. Make certain the damper is closed or the flue is blocked with foam rubber so they do not fall into the fireplace again. If they are not completely feathered or their eyes are not open,

the process of returning the young to their parents will be considerably more difficult.

Because the designs of fireplaces and chimneys are so diverse, there is no single solution that will be appropriate in every instance of a fallen nest. Replacing the nest may require considerable innovation and may not actually be possible. However, there are several options that should be explored. The most important thing to remember is that if the babies are not replaced in the original nest chimney—in approximately the original position in the chimney—the parents will be unable to feed them. At the very least, the nest must be replaced above the damper in the lower section of the chimney.

One option is to place the nest in a shallow wicker basket, which should be set on the smoke

A fallen Chimney Swift nest. The most common cause of mortality in young Chimney Swifts is fallen nests. By keeping the chimney free of creosote buildup, homeowners help assure successful nest building and decrease the chances of the nest falling before the birds have fledged.

shelf just above the damper. The basket must be either weighted or wedged in such a way that when the parents land on it to feed their young, it does not tip over. Some rescuers have placed the nest in a basket and lowered it into the bottom of the chimney from above. Others have had good results taping the nest or a basket to a broom and wedging the broom in a corner of the chimney above the damper.

If it is impossible to return young Chimney Swifts to their parents, they will need to be taken to a licensed wildlife rehabilitator. In the interim, providing proper temporary housing is essential. Because of their lifestyle, Chimney Swifts need to be able to cling to a stable surface to feel secure. The babies will need to be placed in an artificial nest consisting of a small covered box lined with a snag-free cloth. The birds' claws may become tangled in loosely woven fabrics such as terry cloth. An old cotton T-shirt works very well. Do not attempt to feed or give water to baby Chimney Swifts. They are reasonably durable and can fare very well if kept warm, dark, and quiet until they can be taken to a qualified caregiver. However, the sooner they receive care, the more likely they will be to survive the ordeal of being separated from their parents. Your state parks and wildlife department, game warden, or department of natural resources should be able to help you find an individual or facility that can help.

Creating
New
Habitat

The Chimney Swift Towers of Chaetura Canyon

BEGINNING IN 1989, we gradually turned our eight-acre homestead into a Chimney Swift observatory and research station. By late spring 2002, there were twelve towers representing eight different designs scattered across the property. The larger structures hosted roosts of more than one hundred birds annually. Most of the towers attracted nesting swifts—likely because of the established roosts. During the summer months, there was hardly a place on the property where we could not see or hear adult Chimney Swifts overhead or listen to hungry babies calling as they were being fed by their attentive parents. This small piece of Texas Hill Country, dominated by *Chaetura pelagica* activity, had become Chaetura Canyon.

The Observation Towers

The first Chimney Swift towers we built stood 22 ft. tall and measured 18½×18 in. inside. A framework of 2 × 4 in. lumber was covered inside and out with a rough-textured ⅝ in. plywood siding known as Textured One-Eleven (T1-11). We chose a product with deep grooves spaced every 4 in. The 4 × 8 ft. sheets were cut into sections and installed with the grooves running horizontally to provide footholds for the clinging swifts.

We constructed a small access door on the bottom wall of each tower that was just large enough for one of us to squeeze through. The towers were erected 2 ft. from the east side of our two-story house and were spaced 14 ft. apart. They protruded through the overhanging eaves and extended some 5 ft. above the roof. A walkway was built on the second-story level between the towers and the house. Concave Plexiglas viewing ports were installed along the walkway on the second-story tower walls facing the house. The viewing ports were located 13 ft. above the floors of the towers and were shaded by the eaves of the house. By leaning into a port, we could observe the entire interior of each tower. The towers were com-

The house at Chaetura Canyon. The authors' house has two 22 ft. tall Chimney Swift towers built onto the east side. Viewing ports and miniature cameras on the second story allow observation of nesting Chimney Swifts in the towers without interrupting the birds' behavior.

pleted in late April, and we did not have to wait
long before the first Chimney Swifts enthusiasti-
cally investigated our handiwork.

Swifts first entered the North Tower on May
25. The works of earlier observers forewarned that
Chimney Swifts could be easily "spooked" in the
first stages of site acquisition and nest construction and might abandon the site altogether if un-
duly disturbed. Therefore, we refrained from any
use of the viewing ports until several weeks after
the swifts had arrived and taken possession of the
tower. When we could no longer contain our curiosity, we risked a peek into the viewing port
during midday. We saw two Chimney Swifts clinging side by side on the inside north wall. They were
approximately seven feet from the floor, and there
were several "test sticks" glued to the wall just
above them. To our amazement, they were not
startled, and after a few moments they began to
preen. It was then that we noticed that one of the
birds was wearing a small, silvery band on its
right leg.

We returned downstairs and contemplated
what we had seen. Another bander might have
placed the band on the bird. That would have been
remarkable because very few people had been
banding Chimney Swifts in the recent past. The
other possibility was that the banded bird in the
tower was one of our hand-reared swifts that had
made at least one successful migratory round-trip
to South America and back to its foster home. It
would be a couple of very long weeks before we
could even consider capturing the birds so we
could read the number on the band. The suspense
added greatly to our diligence in recording our
observations in the tower.

When the pair's nestlings were twelve days old,
we captured the adults as they were leaving the

tower at dawn. We finally discovered the identity of the banded swift. It was, indeed, one of our hand-reared birds. It had come to us as a five-day-old nestling that had been displaced from its nest chimney in Austin, Texas, the year before. As was the case with all the fifteen hundred Chimney Swifts that came into our care between 1983 and 1999, it had been hand-fed every hour, twelve hours per day until it was five weeks old and ready for release. In subsequent years, we were able to document postrelease survival of several hand-reared Chimney Swifts that used the observation towers for nesting and roosting. One individual was discovered nesting in the South Tower eight years after it was released.

That first fall, the North Tower brought unexpected rewards. Once the nestlings fledged, additional swifts began to join the family to roost at night. Just prior to fall migration, dozens of Chimney Swifts were gathering at dusk in their characteristic circling above the tower. The North Tower went on to host a nesting pair and fall roost every year. Beginning the following year, the South Tower was also occupied annually. Over the next decade and beyond, we documented roosts of over 150 birds and several second broods in the observation towers. Using an infrared light source, we were able to observe, document, and record nocturnal roost behavior.

The Castle

As we contemplated our own mortality and our desire to provide habitat for Chimney Swifts that would endure beyond our lives, we began to consider construction materials that would be more permanent than wood. We found inspiration in the small Central Texas community of Jonestown.

Jonestown cistern.

On a lot just one block off the highway, behind a family-owned business, stands an ancient, cylindrical concrete cistern. It measures 10 ft. in diameter and stands 16 ft. tall. It was originally designed to hold rainwater but has long since ceased to be waterproof. Although it no longer holds water, it does hold an impressive number of Chimney Swifts. The Jonestown cistern is host to hundreds—even thousands—of migrating and nonbreeding Chimney Swifts. On one late summer evening, we counted more than fifteen hundred entering the cistern. Appearing first as tiny specks in the sky, the congregating swifts arrived just before dusk. As the light began to fade and more swifts arrived, they begin to circle lower and lower while chippering loudly. At the time when they actually began to enter the cistern, they swooped low over the surrounding property, within inches of our heads. After fifteen to twenty minutes, all of the circling swifts had gone to roost, leaving the sky as quiet as it was dark. We smiled to ourselves, looked at one another, and wordlessly agreed: "We need a concrete Chimney Swift roost!"

The Jonestown cistern was apparently constructed by pouring several stacked rings of formed concrete. We opted to use 8 in. thick, hollow concrete cinder blocks to construct our roost. It would not be as large as the cistern, but it was going to be bigger than anything we had previously built for Chimney Swifts. The tower itself measures 48 × 48 in. × 12 ft. tall on the outside and 32 × 32 in. × 12 ft. tall on the inside. It was originally left open all the way to the top. It was fitted with a door that had a row of 3 in. ventilation holes along the bottom, backed with ½ × ½ in. galvanized hardware cloth to exclude snakes and other small predators. A locking latch was installed to prevent unauthorized human access.

We began construction of the Castle on May 29, 1994—well after the swifts had returned to select nesting sites for the season. We did not expect there to be any immediate interest in the structure by the local swifts. However, at the end of a day when we had just completed enough of the tower to install the door frame and were walking away from the construction site, we paused to look back at our progress. To our wonder and delight, we observed a lone Chimney Swift dive into the top of the now 6 ft. tall tower and exit through the door opening! It seemed as if it had been watching our progress and just could not wait to make a closer inspection. We completed the construction in late June.

In the spring of the next year, a pair of swifts took up residence and began nest construction on

The Castle. The Castle is a 12 ft. tall cinder-block Chimney Swift tower that has been used as a nest and roost site by Chimney Swifts since its completion in 1994.

the east wall of the Castle. However, the season was to present several disappointments that resulted in a number of modifications to the original design. The swifts laid five eggs and began incubation. When twenty-one days of incubation had passed and the eggs had not yet hatched, we became concerned that something was amiss. We investigated further and found that because the tower was completely open all the way to the top, direct sunlight was able to hit the nest and the eggs during midday. After twelve more days of incubation, the eggs had still not hatched—they had been baked by the sun. We removed the eggs and installed a make-shift plywood top for the tower that reduced the opening to 16 × 16 in. on the north top edge, effectively limiting the amount of sun that could enter the tower. Within a few days, the resident pair of swifts laid more eggs. The second clutch of four eggs all hatched on schedule.

When the nestlings were ten days old, the nest peeled loose from the wall and fell to the floor of the tower. The babies continued to hold tightly to the nest, and fortunately none were injured. We used plastic strapping tape to reattach the nest to the wall in the original location. The parents readily returned and continued to feed their young.

The nestlings thrived and soon began to attempt to leave the nest by climbing onto the inside wall of the tower. They ran into trouble when they were unable to secure a grip on the slick strapping tape that was used to reattach their fallen nest to the wall. At this point, we attached a piece of adhesive-backed felt over the tape to provide the youngsters with a textured surface they could grasp with their claws. Finally, with their sunshade, tape-reinforced nest, and carpeted wall, they were able to proceed with their normal development and fledged from the Castle in the standard amount of time.

Although a considerable amount of intervention was required, the second brood of young Chimney Swifts in the Castle was successful. The design flaws that were discovered and corrected during the first season led to following seasons where no intervention was required. The reduced opening in the top prevented direct sunlight from hitting any eggs laid in subsequent years. The temporary plywood top was later replaced with a reinforced concrete roof with a 16 × 16 in. opening.

Cinder block has proven to be an excellent tower construction medium due to its rough texture, which is easy for the swifts to grasp. However, the surface of cinder block is "crumbly," making a poor surface for attaching the swifts' nests. We corrected this problem by coating the inside walls with a latex (water-based) masonry sealer. This stabilized the surface while retaining the rough texture of the material. We have since learned that this coating needs to be reapplied every year.

The Castle has produced a successful brood and simultaneously hosted a summer roost of thirty to more than one hundred swifts every year since its construction. Fall roosts have also usually consisted of more than one hundred Chimney Swifts.

Thinking and Building Small

Like Althea Sherman's tower, our observation towers and the Castle demonstrated that Chimney Swifts would readily accept structures built specifically for their use. However, these large towers were all rather ambitious projects and not likely to be duplicated in any significant numbers. In 1995, we began experimenting with different building materials and sizes of towers. Our objective was to design a tower that was large enough to accommodate the swifts' needs, yet small enough that it could be built by the average, do-it-yourself homeowner. Our inspiration came from some unexpected and unlikely sources.

The Prism Tower

One summer day as we were driving through Dripping Springs, Texas, our eyes were drawn to the signage for a small shopping center. Rising out of the asphalt parking lot was a three-sided plywood column supported by three steel legs. Signs for

An "accidental" Chimney Swift tower. This 16 ft. tower was made by bolting two 4 x 8 ft. sheets of plywood siding to each side of a triangular welded-steel frame.

each of the tenants in the shopping center were attached to the outside of the tower.

When we pulled in to investigate the structure, we noted that there was no bottom or top and that there were bird droppings on the asphalt between the tower legs. Looking from the bottom, up into the column, we saw a Chimney Swift nest and several young swifts clinging to the inside wall—looking back at us. This 16 ft. "accidental" Chimney Swift tower was made by bolting two 4 × 8 ft. sheets of plywood siding to each side of a triangular welded-steel frame.

Inspired by this simple design, we decided to build a smaller version and hope for the swifts to test it. "The Prism Tower," as we dubbed it, went through several early modifications that resulted in an 8 ft. tall, vinyl-sided tower with interior panels of T1-11 plywood siding.

Once the design was perfected, the Prism Tower produced a healthy brood of Chimney Swifts every year. Frequently, a second brood succeeded as well.

We checked the sign tower in Dripping Springs for Chimney Swift nests for several years after we first discovered it and were never disappointed. However, one day in the winter of 2001, we were dismayed to see that the tower had been removed. The following spring, swifts were observed flying low around the area where the tower—their "home"—had once stood.

The Field Towers

Prompted by the success of the 8 ft. Prism Tower, we designed a more easily constructed four-sided tower. In the small field behind our house, we performed a temperature experiment with this new design. We built two small towers 10 ft. and 20 ft. due east of the Prism Tower. Both measured 14 ½ × 14 ½ in. inside and stood 11 ft. tall—8 ft. of tower on 3 ft. supporting legs. Both had 11 × 7 in. top openings and were constructed with the inside and outside walls separated by a ¾ in. space. In one tower, the space was left as an empty air space; in the other, the space was filled with ¾ in. foil-backed insulation. Over the summer months, the insulated tower was consistently 2°F–3°F cooler inside than the uninsulated one. Every wooden tower that we built from that point on was insulated.

The following year, we made a final improvement to the Field Towers. A 7 in. tall wooden

The Prism and Field Towers. These three designs of 8 ft. tall towers all proved to be acceptable to the swifts, although overheating in the initial design of these smaller towers did present some problems.

extension, or "collar," was placed over the 11 × 7 in. openings of each tower. This further limited the amount of direct sunlight that was able to enter the towers and helped keep the interior of the towers cooler. When the swifts returned, they were undeterred by the remodeling project.

The Pool Towers

This pair of towers was so named because they were constructed next to a small water feature created for the local wildlife. Their experimental purpose was twofold: to test a smaller version of the successful cinder-block Castle and to test the swifts' reaction to potential nesting sites in close proximity to one another.

The Pool Towers both stand on a single concrete slab. The actual tower construction uses 4 in.

The Pool Towers.

thick, hollow concrete cinder blocks. The towers have a 12 in. inside diameter and stand 10 ft. 2 in. tall. The towers are only 26 in. apart and are oriented on a north-south line.

During the construction, while we were actually on the scaffold adding a course of cinder blocks, we thought we saw something drop into the northern tower. When we looked in from the top, we were face-to-face with a Chimney Swift that was holding a stick crosswise in its bill. Over the next few days, as we added cinder blocks to the towers, the swifts added sticks to their nest—the race was on!

Our finishing touches to the towers involved placing some intricate concrete forms on top that temporarily reduced the opening to 6 × 11 in. This proved to be plenty of room for the swifts to enter, so we made the reduction of the opening permanent to provide additional protection from direct sun and rain.

The North Pool Tower has hosted successful nests every year, including the first construction year. Although swifts were occasionally seen entering and even roosting for a few nights in the South Pool Tower, we never found any evidence of nesting. In one of several personal communications, Ralph Dexter told us that many of the suitable air shafts in the buildings of Kent State University did not contain nests. He also noted that the nests tended to be in the outermost shafts— seemingly placing as much distance as possible between nest sites. Apparently, the proximity of other nest sites is an important factor to Chimney Swifts when choosing a home for their young. To date, we have not documented swifts nesting in structures that were closer than 10 ft. apart.

Basics of Tower Construction and Maintenance

CHIMNEY SWIFT TOWERS SHOULD BE built as additional habitat, not as replacements for chimneys being used successfully by nesting and roosting swifts.

The most important lesson we have learned in our search for the perfect Chimney Swift tower is that even the best of our smaller designs to date cannot duplicate the ideal nesting conditions that are provided by a small masonry chimney. Towers present problems of overheating and predator control that are usually not a concern in chimneys.

When towers are being constructed specifically for Chimney Swifts as nesting and roosting sites, the following factors must be taken into account:

Location

Towers should be located in a small clearing at least 10 ft. away from any overhanging tree branches or on the north side of a building, with the top extending at least 4 ft. above the roof to discourage predators such as cats, raccoons, and squirrels from jumping to the top of the tower.

Size

Small towers (8–12 ft. tall with 14–18 in. inside diameter) are suitable for use as nest sites. Larger

Swifts over a roost at dusk.
Courtesy John D. Ingram

towers are also more likely to be used as roosts by substantial numbers of nonbreeding and migratory Chimney Swifts.

Diameter

The tower must be large enough in diameter for the swifts to be able to fly up and down inside the structure. Although some experimental 12 in. cinder-block towers have been successful, we now consider a 14 in. minimum inside diameter to be preferable in wooden towers. Wooden towers must be larger to compensate for their susceptibility to overheating.

Height

The tower must be deep enough to provide protection of the nest from direct sunlight: 8 ft. minimum inside depth.

Top Opening

The width of the opening of the top of the tower should be no more than half the inside diameter. The opening should be situated on the north top edge of the tower to limit the amount of rain and direct sunlight that can penetrate the interior of the tower. For example, the top opening for a 14 × 14 in. tower should be no greater than 7 × 14 in. No opening should be less than 6 × 11 in.

Insulation

Because Chimney Swift towers are not surrounded by a house as regular chimneys are, they are subject to overheating. We highly recommend using double-walled structures to minimize this problem.

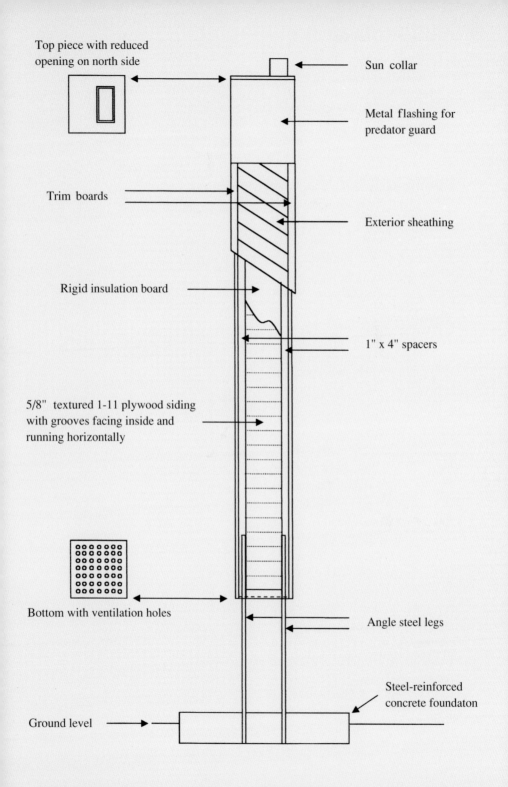

Top piece with reduced opening on north side

Sun collar

Metal flashing for predator guard

Trim boards

Exterior sheathing

Rigid insulation board

1" x 4" spacers

5/8" textured 1-11 plywood siding with grooves facing inside and running horizontally

Bottom with ventilation holes

Angle steel legs

Steel-reinforced concrete foundaton

Ground level

This means that the nest chamber should be separated from the outside wall by an insulated space. This space should be a minimum of 3/4 in. and filled with 3/4 in. rigid insulation board.

Inside Material

The inside vertical surface must be textured enough for the swifts to be able to cling to it. Rough-textured exterior wood siding, cinder block, textured concrete, or rough-textured stucco will work well.

Outside Material

The outside material must be durable, heat reflective, and difficult for predators to climb: smooth textured and light in color.

Constructing even a small Chimney Swift tower requires a considerable investment of time and resources. However, when a pair of swifts accepts one of these structures, it will become much more than just a nest box for raising their young. Unlike may other species of cavity-nesting birds that abandon the nest site when the nestlings fledge, Chimney Swifts continue to use their chosen site as a nightly roost throughout the spring and summer and into the fall. It also serves as a refuge from inclement weather and a safe place to rest when summer heat is intense or when flying insect food is scarce; it is literally their only terrestrial contact. In a very real sense, an occupied tower will become "home" to the resident birds during their entire six- to seven-month stay in North America. Some particularly appealing towers may become summer roosts for extended families and large groups of nonbreeding birds or even congregation sites for migrating swifts in spring and fall.

Tower Maintenance

During the summer nesting season, efforts should be made to keep vegetation low around the tower foundation. Tall grasses and other plants that come into contact with the tower can provide "highways" for ants. If a tower is built on legs, a 2–3 in. band of sticky insect barrier such as Tanglefoot should be applied to each leg near the base of the tower. It should be inspected several times during the nesting season for effectiveness. In towers that are in direct ground contact, a dusting of diatomaceous earth or 5 percent Sevin dust around the outside base of the tower will help keep ants away from the nest. Treatment will need to be reapplied periodically, and especially after rainstorms.

In the fall, after the Chimney Swifts have migrated south and are no longer using the tower, the bottom should be cleaned of droppings, eggshells, and other material. The nest from each season should also be removed before the swifts return. Although Chimney Swifts have been observed reusing old nests, these nests will not be as strong and secure as a newly constructed nest, and nest building seems to be an important part of pair bonding in Chimney Swifts. When replacing the bottom of a freestanding tower, make certain that the bottom is securely reattached.

The exterior of towers that are sided with wood will need to be repainted every few years, either before the swifts arrive or after they leave. Covering the top during the winter will extend the life of wooden towers. The interior of cinder-block towers will need to be retreated with a latex-based sealer every year.

Monitoring Nest and Roost Sites

WE OFTEN SAY THAT OBSERVING Chimney Swifts is "a pain in the neck." This is literally true because most of their activity takes place high above treetop level. One must be constantly looking up to observe the swifts' "kiting," "V-ing," "cracking-the-whip," "parading," and feeding maneuvers.

If observing Chimney Swifts in the open sky is difficult, observing them in the nest or roost site is nearly impossible without the use of electronic surveillance equipment. Even if direct access is possible, too much interference (or *any* interference at the wrong time) may cause the swifts to abandon the site. Fortunately, there are several ways to know what is transpiring in a chimney or tower without ever looking inside while the swifts are in residence.

Actually seeing a single Chimney Swift enter a site during the day is a chance event at best, especially early in the season. The best time and place to observe swifts around their home is at dusk and from a distance.

If swifts are suspected or known to occupy a structure, patiently and quietly observe from at least thirty feet away. Arrive approximately thirty minutes before sunset. Most weather forecasts include time of sunset in their daily report. Pair bonding begins soon after the return of the swifts to their breeding area from their South American wintering grounds, so groups of two to five or more

birds will fly in tight formation, uttering their staccato, chippering vocalizations. A mated pair will reveal themselves when they both snap their wings up into a stationary "V" position and glide one behind the other. Swifts will generally make several passes and circle the structure before entering. Many birds have unique postures when tumbling from the sky, which can be very entertaining for the observer.

Roosting structures may contain as few as a dozen or as many as several thousand Chimney Swifts. Generally, roosting birds arrive in "waves." The first arrivals will circle the area, foraging and vocalizing before entering. Additional birds will continue to arrive, circle, and enter the structure as dusk falls. Observers who are interested in counting swifts should monitor the sky until dark, counting individual birds as they enter the site. We have found that a hand-held athletic lap counter works well for counting individuals in roosts of up to two hundred birds. Larger roosts require some estimating. An effective method is to count birds in fives or tens as they enter a site. A lap counter can still be effective. The number indicated on the counter can be multiplied for a reasonably accurate estimate.

Chimney Swift vocalizations also offer aid in determining the activity in and around a structure.

Inside a nesting structure, mated birds will utter soft chippering calls. Occasionally, the sound of their wings as they fly up and down the interior can be heard from outside. Very excited and loud chippering accompanied by a clapping sound as the swifts snap their wings usually denotes aggression or a territorial dispute.

Nestling swifts produce at least two different calls, which usually become audible from outside the structure after the birds reach ten days of age. The raucous chatter they produce each time an adult enters indicates that the young are being fed. A mechanical, rasping call indicates fear or agitation. Hearing either call indicates an active nest.

After Chimney Swifts have migrated from the area in the fall, an inspection of the bottom of the nest site can be very informative. The shear volume of droppings can indicate whether the site was occupied by a few or many swifts. When dried, the average droppings produced by a family of five or six Chimney Swifts during their summer stay will fill a one-quart plastic bag. Also, Chimney Swift parents remove eggshells from the nest just as songbirds do. However, they do not carry them away. Instead, they just toss the shells over the edge of the nest, and they collect on the bottom of the tower. A hatchling emerges from the egg by breaking completely through the shell. Half shells indicate a successful hatching. Unevenly broken segments of shell usually indicate a fallen egg. All pieces of eggshell will have a leathery appearance.

Bits of material used for nesting, as well as the construction of the nest, can be examined. It is sometimes possible to identify the favorite species of tree that was used. Hardened threads of translucent saliva that hold the nest together will be clearly visible. The entire old nest can and should be removed.

Conserving and Building for the Future

The Kiosk Tower at
Granite Shoals
Elementary School.

MANY OF THE TRADITIONAL SITES used by Chimney Swifts are old by our modern standards and in danger of being removed to make way for new construction projects. In some cases, these structures can be identified for their importance to migratory birds and conserved. Perhaps one of the most notable examples can be found in Wolfville, Nova Scotia. Once part of a dairy processing facility, the chimney was scheduled for demolition in 1989 along with the building to which it was attached. The chimney was saved by cooperative efforts of the Blomidin Naturalists Society and the Wolfville Business Development Corporation. Combining the conservation of an old site with some innovative new construction created the Robie Tufts Nature Center. A covered pavilion was erected around the chimney, and interpretive information was placed on the walls of a small enclosure that surrounds the base of the chimney. The efforts of many volunteers and local groups ensured that Chimney Swifts continue to have a safe place to roost in what is one of the most northern reaches of their range in North America.

With few exceptions, the widespread creation of Chimney Swift nesting and roosting habitat has been "accidental" and a result of standard human

Robie Tufts Nature Center. This nature center is the result of conservation efforts to save a historical Chimney Swift roost that was scheduled to be demolished in 1989.
Courtesy Jim Wolford

construction practices over the last two centuries. However, where masonry chimneys and fireplaces were once standard, pre-fabricated stainless steel units have now become the norm. Large air shafts that once served to cool multistory urban buildings are no longer necessary now that central air-conditioning is common. Currently, there does not seem to be any standard construction that is likely to automatically produce any significant number of new Chimney Swift nest or roost sites. However, there are many "missed opportunities" in Chimney Swift conservation.

Modern architecture commonly includes aesthetic features along with the practical. When these features are expressed in the form of columns and towers, Chimney Swift habitat may be ready-made. Because these features are often detached from the main structure and not functional, the conflicts that frequently arise between Chimney

Swifts and people are no longer an issue. Any structure that is tall, hollow, open at the top, and roughly textured inside is probable Chimney Swift habitat. In many cases, a few very simple changes during the design phase of some projects can create structures that are suitable for Chimney Swifts and pleasing to humans. This may be especially appropriate in projects that are already involved in wildlife and nature education. The Lower Colorado River Authority (LCRA) in Central Texas has successfully executed this concept at their Muleshoe Bend Recreational Area. At the entrance of the park, the LCRA designed and constructed a 12 ft. tall column made of natural rock. The native stone feature was built to hold a lighting fixture but has a hollow center for the benefit of Chimney Swifts. Educational materials about Chimney Swifts are distributed, and there are plans to provide interpretive talks about the structure.

Architectural features. Modern architecture commonly includes aesthetic features along with the practical. When these features are expressed in the form of columns and towers, Chimney Swift habitat may be ready-made. By taking advantage of missed opportunities, builders could provide countless new nesting and roosting sites.

Muleshoe Bend Tower. The Lower Colorado River Authority in Central Texas successfully executed this concept at their Muleshoe Bend Recreational Area. At the entrance to the park, the LCRA designed and constructed a 12 ft. tall feature made of natural rock. The native stone structure was built to hold a lighting fixture but has a hollow center for the benefit of Chimney Swifts.

Every city, county, state, and national park uses kiosks to provide information for its visitors. Even many housing developments incorporate nature and jogging trails into their communities. With this in mind, we designed a "Kiosk Chimney Swift Tower," a miniature version of the Nova Scotia tower. Simply put, the Kiosk Tower is a 4 x 4 x 8 ft. tall building with a nest tower protruding though the center of the roof. The outer walls provide protection for the nest chamber as well a convenient place to mount visual displays, trail maps, and other materials pertinent to the park.

A prototype Kiosk Tower was installed at the City of Austin's Center for Environmental Education at the Hornsby Bend Wastewater Treatment Plant—a nationally known birding hot spot. The tower was occupied by Chimney Swifts the first season it was in place and hosted a successful nest every year thereafter. It also draws much attention

Why Should I Care about Chimney Swifts?

In the conservation of any species, the question is a fair one. There are basic reasons why everyone should care about the fate of Chimney Swifts.

Every day, Chimney Swifts eat nearly one-third their own weight in flying insects such as mosquitoes, biting flies, and termites. A nest of five noisy Chimney Swift nestlings will be fed as many as twelve thousand insects daily.

Chimney Swifts historically used large, hollow trees for nests and roosts. As the ancient forests were cut down, they learned to use chimneys and other structures instead.

Today, just as Purple Martins do, Chimney Swifts rely almost entirely on human-made structures for nest sites. Because they cannot perch as songbirds do, Chimney Swifts must have deep shafts in which to raise their families and roost at night.

Chimney Swifts are protected by state wildlife codes and federal law under the Migratory Bird Treaty Act of 1916. Violations can result in a maximum penalty of five thousand dollars and/ or six months in jail per count.

Chimney Swifts are declining in numbers, and you can make a difference in their fate.
Like watching a beautiful sunset, observing Chimney Swifts' aerial acrobatics and interactions is a simple pleasure of aesthetic value that nature has to offer.

A Kiosk Tower. The building is 4 × 4 × 8 ft. tall with a 12 ft. nest tower protruding though the center of the roof. The outer walls provide protection for the nest chamber as well a convenient place to mount visual displays, trail maps, and other materials pertinent to the parks in which they are located.

from visiting birders, conservation groups, and curious schoolchildren. The design has since been duplicated in city parks, nature preserves, demonstration farms, and national wildlife refuges.

One of the best examples of the educational possibilities of a Kiosk Tower can be found at the Granite Shoals Elementary School in Central Texas. When the new school was built, students, teachers, parents, and the business community came together to create a nature trail in the adjacent woods. The local wood-shop class had already built numerous nest boxes and bird feeders when the instructor learned about Chimney Swift towers. Because it involved such a variety of skills (concrete and steel work, carpentry, roofing, and painting), the construction of a Kiosk Tower for the trail was adopted as a class project. While the shop class was hard at work on the tower, the second-grade students were busy learning about Chimney Swifts. When the trail was formally dedicated, the young naturalists proudly presented their new knowledge in a program for the rest of the school and the local media. Their informative artwork adorned the display panels of the new Kiosk Tower.

Cinder-block, stucco, and stone walls and fences also provide an opportunity for habitat creation. Such walls require stabilizing columns every few feet. These columns can be built slightly taller than the wall and left hollow and open on top, with drain openings on the bottom. This makes them perfectly acceptable for use by nesting Chimney Swifts. There are even cinder blocks available called "pilasters" that seem to be ideally designed for the job. These blocks measure 16 × 16 × 8 in. tall and have a 12 in. hollow center. Some enterprising conservationists are building such columns at evenly spaced intervals along their fence lines to accommodate Chimney Swifts—much in the same way that bluebird trails have commonly been established in many regions of North America.

Recycled materials may also play a role in the future of Chimney Swift conservation. Piles of old concrete culvert pipes are lying unused in many municipal, county, and state storage yards around the country. Chimney Swifts have been observed nesting in concrete standpipes, so there is no reason to doubt that the birds would use these discarded pipes if they stood upright. Certainly, a foundation and drainage would need to be provided, but no additional construction would be necessary. There might even be an incentive for waste-management facilities to erect rows of these concrete columns around their operations to aid in the control of flying insects.

The opportunities to provide habitat for the adaptable Chimney Swift are limited only by our imagination and initiative. Whether we leave our chimneys open for them to use as they have for generations, organize community efforts to place new Chimney Swift towers in our parks, or simply point to the sky and show someone a Chimney Swift for the first time, we can each make a difference in how this story proceeds. The skies would indeed be empty without the merry sounds and astounding acrobatic displays of the Chimney Swifts.

Cinder-block wall. If left hollow, the stabilizing columns on cinder-block, stucco, and stone walls and fences could provide considerable habitat for Chimney Swifts.

What Can I Do to Help Chimney Swifts?

If you have a masonry or clay flue-tile chimney, keep the top open and the damper closed from March through October to provide a nest site for these insect eaters.

Metal chimneys should be permanently capped to prevent birds and other wildlife from being trapped.

Have your chimney cleaned before the Chimney Swifts return from their winter home in South America.

Work with local conservation groups to construct Chimney Swift towers.

Educate your friends and neighbors about Chimney Swifts.

The Stall and Turn

The Parade

Flight Maneuvers

The Tag

Glossary

ALTRICIAL: Pertaining to young that are hatched blind, naked, and helpless and that require extended parental care

Anisodactyl: Having three toes forward and one toe back

Apodidae: The family to which all true swifts belong

Bill: The jaws and horny covering of a bird's mouth; colloquially known as the "beak"

Bird banding: The process of marking an individual bird by attaching a numbered aluminum band to its leg

Bolus: A mass of food prepared for swallowing

Breeding range: The geographic area in which species attract a mate and raise their young

Brood: A group of young animals

Brooding: The activity of covering the young for the purpose of protecting and/or providing warmth

Chaetura: The genus to which Chimney Swifts belong

Damper: A mechanism for regulating airflow in a fireplace chimney

Ectoparasite: A parasite that lives on the exterior of its host

Egg tooth: A toothlike prominence on the tip of the bill of a bird embryo, which is used to break the eggshell during the hatching process

Feather shaft: The central, rigid portion of a feather

Feather sheath: The thin, translucent cover that encases newly emerging feathers

Feather tract: A special area of the skin of birds from which feathers sprout

Fire screen: A wire-mesh covering on the front of a fireplace designed to keep sparks from escaping into the living space

Fledgling: A young bird that has left the nest but is still dependent on its parents

Flight feathers: The long feathers of the wings that
are used for flight

Flue: The channel above a fireplace for the passage of
smoke

Flue tile: A hollow, masonry clay product used in the
construction of chimney flues

Gape: The distance between the jaws or mandibles of
a bird; the mouth

Hallux: The back digit or toe of the foot

Hatchling: A young bird that has just emerged from
the egg

Histoplasmosis: A lung disease caused by the fungus
Histoplasma capsulatum

Incubation: The act of covering eggs with the body to
provide warmth and promote development of the
embryos

Migratory Bird Treaty Act: An international agree-
ment to protect birds that migrate between the
United States and other countries

Mortar joint: A masonry seam between bricks,
stones, or flue tiles

Nestling: A young bird that has begun to develop
feathers

Passerines: Birds belonging to the order
Passeriformes; perching birds or songbirds

Pinfeather: A feather just beginning to grow through
the skin

Preen: To use the bill to dress, condition, or rearrange
the feathers

Primaries: The long feathers of the wings that are
used for flight

Roost: A place where birds rest or spend the night

Salivary glands: Glands that secrete saliva

Smoke shelf: A relatively flat area located above the
fireplace in some chimneys

Stroboscopic photography: The technique of producing pictures by using flashes of light

Wintering grounds: The geographic area where a
migratory species resides during the non-breeding
period of the year.

Acknowledgments

WE HAVE LEARNED THAT ONE or two individuals can make at least a small difference in the conservation of a species. However, it takes the participation, support, and encouragement of many to bring about significant change. We would like to thank Sam Droege, Chuck Hunter, Madge Lindsay, Cecilia Riley, Cliff Shackelford, and the Texas Parks and Wildlife Department for their help in publishing and distributing our initial Chimney Swift conservation information to the general public. Funding for additional publications as well as for ongoing research and the construction of numerous Chimney Swift towers has been generously provided by the Driftwood Wildlife Association and its loyal membership, the Travis Audubon Society, the Peterson Charitable Lead Trust, Carol Cassetti, Dr. Evelyn Bull, and the many research associates in the North American Chimney Swift Nest Site Research Project.

We are indebted to Mike Quinn for his assistance in the identification of insects that are taken by Chimney Swifts and to Paul Hempel for his public relations efforts in the professional chimney-sweeping industry on behalf of Chimney Swifts.

For access to all of the modern technology that was not available to our predecessors in Chimney Swift research, we will be forever indebted to Mel Rinn, our personal "Mr. Wizard." Mel was on twenty-four-hour call to answer our endless questions about computers, webcams, and the Internet. He designed and built the infrared emitters that allowed us to witness portions of the swifts' lives that have never before been documented—all without any disturbance to the swifts.

Considerable moral support and fresh insight have been provided by Chimney Swift rehabilitator and conservationist Joyce Rosson.

For their personal encouragement and support over the past twenty years and extremely helpful comments and suggestions on an early draft of the manuscript, we are grateful to Ann Connell, Don Connell, Steve Janda, and Kathy McElveen.

Dr. Richard B. Fischer has been a personal inspiration throughout our ongoing love affair with Chimney Swifts, and he has graciously provided assistance with the manuscript. Dr. Fischer also gave permission to quote from his writings and to use some of his original photos from his extensive fourteen-year study of Chimney Swifts.

Permission to quote from other publications was granted by the Iowa University Press. Additional photographs were provided by the Oberlin College Archives, John Ingram, Nancy Whitworth, Jim Wolford, Kent State University, and the Texas Parks and Wildlife Department. The final version of the range map was created by Susan Supple with assistance from Leah Linney.

Special thanks are due to our editor, Shannon Davies, who encouraged us to share our knowledge about and love of these wonderful birds with a wider audience through this book.

Finally, we wish to acknowledge Dr. Ralph W. Dexter. When we were just beginning to study the fascinating biology of Chimney Swifts, Dr. Dexter was coming to the end of a lifetime of Chimney Swift research. In spite of our inexperience, he treated us as colleagues and inspired us with his dedication and support. We miss Ralph, and we fondly dedicate this book to his memory.

Paul D. Kyle and Georgean Z. Kyle

References

AUDUBON, John J. 1840. The Chimney Swallow or American Swift. In *The Birds of America,* vol. 1., 164–69. New York: J. J. Audubon.

Bent, Arthur C. 1940. Chimney Swift. In *Life Histories of North American Cuckoos, Goatsuckers, Hummingbirds and Their Allies,* 271–93. Toronto, Ontario, Canada: General Publishing Company.

Chantler, Phil, and Gerald Driessens. 1995. Chimney Swift. In *Swifts: A Guide to Swifts and Treeswifts of the World,* 166–67. The Banks, Mountfield, East Sussex, England: Pica Press.

Cink, Calvin L., and Charles T. Collins. 2002. Chimney Swift (*Chaetura pelagica*). In *The Birds of North America,* no. 646, ed. A. Poole and F. Gill. Philadelphia: The Birds of North America.

Coffey, Ben B., Jr. 1944. Winter home of Chimney Swifts discovered in northeastern Peru. *The Migrant* 15(3):37–38.

Dexter, Ralph W. 1946. More concerning the thundering and clapping sounds of the Chimney Swift. *Auk* 63(3):439–40.

———. 1952. Extra parental cooperation in the nesting of Chimney Swifts. *Wilson Bulletin* 64(3):133–39.

———. 1979. Fourteen-year life history of a banded Chimney Swift. *Bird-Banding* 50(1):30–33.

Fischer, Richard B. 1958. The breeding biology of the Chimney Swift *Chaetura pelagica* (*Linnaeus*). New York State Museum and Science Service Bulletin 368. Albany: University of the State of New York.

Ganier, Albert F. 1944. More about the Chimney Swifts found in Peru. *The Migrant* 15(3):39–41.

Kyle, Paul D., and Georgean Z. 1989–2002. Chimney Swift research. In *Annual Report.* Driftwood, Tex.: Driftwood Wildlife Association.

————. 1990. An evaluation of the role of microbial flora in the saliva transfer technique of hand-rearing Chimney Swifts (*Chaetura pelagica*). In *Wildlife Rehabilitation,* vol. 8, ed. D. Ludwig, 65–72. Edina, Minn.: Burgess Printing Company.

————. 1995a. Breeding success of a hand-reared Chimney Swift (*Chaetura pelagica*): A case history. In *Wildlife Rehabilitation,* vol. 13, ed. D. Ludwig, 131–37. Edina, Minn.: Burgess Printing Company.

————. 1995b. *Environmental Tips for Professional Chimney Sweeps.* PWD BR W7100-2465A. Austin: Texas Parks and Wildlife Department.

————. 1995c. Hand-rearing Chimney Swifts (*Chaetura pelagica*): A 12-year retrospective. In *Wildlife Rehabilitation,* vol. 13, ed. D. Ludwig, 95–121. Edina, Minn.: Burgess Printing Company.

————. 1996–2002. *Chaetura,* vols. 1– 7. Austin, Tex.: Driftwood Wildlife Association.

————. 1998. *Providing and Maintaining Nesting Habitat for Chimney Swifts: A Guide for Homeowners.* PWD BR W7000-246. Austin: Texas Parks and Wildlife Department.

————. 2002. *Rehabilitation and Conservation of Chimney Swifts* (Chaetura pelagica). 3d ed. Driftwood, Tex.: Driftwood Wildlife Association.

Lincoln, Frederick C. 1944. Chimney Swift's winter home discovered. *Auk* 61:604–9.

Sauer, J. R., B. G. Peterjohn, S. Schwartz, and J. E. Hines. 1996. *The North American Breeding Bird Survey Home Page.* Version 95.1. Laurel, Md.: Patuxent Wildlife Research Center.

Saville, A. C. 1950. The flight mechanisms of swifts and hummingbirds. *Auk* 67:499–504.

Sherman, Althea R. 1952. Home life of the Chimney Swift. In *Birds of an Iowa Dooryard,* ed. Fred J. Pierce, 40–61. Boston: Christopher Publishing House.

Terres, John K. 1982. *The Audubon Society Encyclopedia of North American Birds.* New York: Alfred A. Knopf.

Whittemore, Margaret. 1981. *Chimney Swifts and Their Relatives.* Jackson, Miss.: Nature Book Publishers.

Index